TALKING WITH COUPLES

TALKING WITH COUPLES

PSYCHOANALYTIC PSYCHOTHERAPY
OF THE COUPLE RELATIONSHIP

by

*Giulio Cesare Zavattini, Barbara Bianchini,
Marina Capello, Laura Dallanegra,
Maria Adelaide Lupinacci, Fabio Monguzzi,
and Lidia Vitalini*

published for

The Harris Meltzer Trust

by

KARNAC

Published for The Harris Meltzer Trust by
Karnac Books Ltd, 118 Finchley Road, London NW3 5HT

First published in Italian as *Parlando con la Coppia: Psicoterapia Psicoanalitica della Relazione di Coppia* by Edizioni Borla, Rome.
Copyright © 2013 Edizioni Borla with Giulio Cesare Zavattini, Barbara Bianchini, Marina Capello, Laura Dallanegra, Maria Adelaide Lupinacci, Fabio Monguzzi, Lidia Vitalini

Copyright © 2015 The Harris Meltzer Trust
Translation by Giuliana Majo

British Library Cataloguing in Publication Data
A C.I.P. for this book is available from the British Library

ISBN 978 1 78220 1175

Edited, designed and produced by The Bourne Studios
www.bournestudios.co.uk
Printed in Great Britain by TJ International Ltd, Padstow, Cornwall

www.harris-meltzer-trust.org.uk
www.karnacbooks.com

CONTENTS

v

INTRODUCTION

Barbara Bianchini is a psychologist and psychoanalytic psycho-therapist, working privately with individuals, couples and groups. She is a full member of the British Society of Couple Psychotherapists and Counsellors (BSCPC), a member of the International Association of Couple and Family Psychoanalysis (IACFP), the *Associazione di Psicoterapia Psicoanalitica di Gruppo* (APG), and the *Confederazione delle Organizzazioni Italiane per la ricerca Analitica sui Gruppi* (COIRAG), where she teaches psychotherapy. She has been honorary judge at the Milan Court of Appeal in the children and minors section, and a consultant at the ASL Couple and Family Centre in Milan.

Marina Capello is a psychologist and psychoanalytic psycho-therapist, working privately with adults, adolescents, and couples. She works in the legal field as outpatient psychologist at the *Servizio Dipendenze nella Casa di Reclusione di Milano-Opera* and as external advisor for the Ministry of Justice at the *Ufficio Esecuzione Penale Esterna* (UEPE) of Milan and Lodi, where she conducts training courses and supervision groups with psychologists and social workers.

Laura Dallanegra is a psychologist and psychoanalytic psychotherapist, working privately with adults, adolescents, and couples, and as a supervisor of clinical cases. She teaches the theory and clinical technique of couple psychotherapy. She was a founder member of the *Ambulatorio dell'Associazione* (Area G) in Milan, and a member of the training committee of the *Scuola di Psicoterapia* (Area G). She has been a consultant at the Couple and Family Centre (ASL) in Milan.

Maria Adelaide Lupinacci is a psychoanalyst and psychiatrist, a member of the Italian Psychoanalytic Society (SPI) and the IPA. She specialises in the psychoanalysis of children and adolescents. She was secretary of the SPI commission on the analysis of children and adolescents, and of the *Centri di Psicoanalisi* in Rome. She is author of many papers on the early Oedipus complex, countertransference, guilt, the mind's space-time, and psychoanalytic psychotherapy of the couple. She works privately in Rome with adults, adolescents, children and couples.

Fabio Monguzzi is a psychologist and psychoanalytic psychotherapist, now in private practice after working with various health institutions in the public sector. He is affiliated to the *Associazione per la Ricerca in Psicologia Clinica* (ARP) and honorary Judge at the Milan juvenile court. He is a full member of the British Society of Couple Psychotherapists and Counsellors (BSCPC) and a member of the International Association of Couple and Family Psychoanalysis (IACFP).

Lidia Vitalini is a psychologist and psychoanalytic psychotherapist, and a member of *Metandro*, which provides medical and psychological services for children from the age of one to four. She works privately with adults, adolescents and couples.

Giulio Cesare Zavattini is professor of assessment and intervention in clinical psychodynamic work with couples at the Sapienza University of Rome. He is a full member of the British Society of Couple Psychotherapists and Counsellors (BSCPC) and of the International Association of Couple and Family Psychoanalysis (IACFP), and a member of the international advisory board of the journal *Couple and Family Psychoanalysis*. With Renata Tambelli he is editor of the Borla series *Psicoanalisi e Relazioni: Studi su Individuo, Coppia e Famiglia*.

The purpose of this book is to share the educational and experiential journey of a group of psychoanalytic psychotherapists who have for some years been working with families and individuals in both the private and the public sector. The members of the group, who come from similar theoretical perspectives (in object relations), share the view that clinical experience is the fundamental point of departure for their own professional and personal development. The group was designed to create an environment for study, debate and comparison of the psychological, relational and social dynamics that contribute to the functioning of a couple or a family.

The activities of the group take place on two fronts: on the one hand, clinical work with couples and families, and on the other, theoretical formulation and review in study and supervision groups, professional development courses, and seminars hosting visiting experts from Italy and other countries. An educational programme has become established which includes professional development courses lasting up to four years, that are open also to professionals in the psychology sector, and facilitated and supported by Professor Giulio Cesare Zavattini, director of the clinical course on psychodynamic work with couples at the Sapienza University in Rome. These courses have stimulated a gradual and progressive interest in the deeper understanding of the theoretical basis and clinical functioning of such work, which in turn has inspired the writing of this book.

The programme has led to a rewarding exchange with other researchers and interpreters of couple and family psychoanalytic dynamics, such as members of the Italian Psychoanalytic Society (SPI) and the British Society of Couple Psychotherapists and

Counsellors (BSCPC) in London. Many experienced colleagues have been invited to become involved with the Centre's work groups, and their contributions in organising seminars and professional training have been invaluable. In this respect we particularly thank our guests Diana Norsa, Carlos Tabbia, and David Hewison.

The collaboration with foreign researchers has revealed disparate, though not opposing, theoretical languages and points of view. Extending our contacts to other groups and perspectives has been fruitful in expanding our knowledge and in defining a theoretical–technical working model for couples and families that we find useful in our relationship with our patients.

The psychotherapeutic and consultative experience that we have had within the public sector, working in Milan, has proved very important at a clinical level. The experience of our group members in consultations over a long period at family therapy centres, which encompass a wide spectrum of encounters and relationships, indicated a need to expand the field of operation and availability, especially since in times of crisis the demand for help increases. Moreover the limitations imposed by the resources of the public health sector have led therapists to find new ways of adapting their psychoanalytic techniques and methods to suit the realistic capacities of these institutions.

Another important contribution to the experience of the members has been the opportunity to be part of a legal environment – a multitude of difficulties associated with different types of families resulting at times in the role of honorary judge. In recent times, families have evolved within a diverse social landscape: mixed couples, different cultures, and also, extended family systems or single parent situations which can make social integration harder. The responsibility, although shared, to choose and think of the best way to resolve legal issues, has made us acutely aware of the powerful impact which these choices can have on the life of the people involved. Members have become much more aware of the complexity of their professional role in enabling the process of separation or divorce, which is often riddled with controversies and sometimes become quite violent, but also entails witnessing the delicacy of the nature of child care decisions and parenting.

In addition to this, some members have accrued a great deal of experience from many years of teaching theory and techniques of psychoanalytic psychotherapy with couples in training institutions. The experience of transmitting knowledge to new generations of psychologists and keeping an eye on the evolution of theoretical models has allowed continuous exchange and feedback. It has demonstrated to us the extent of the interest in the subject and the relevance of achieving a serious and adequate understanding of the couple relationship in its varying contexts.

The interchange between the areas of work and the work discussion groups has shown itself to be of fundamental importance in stimulating not only professional but also the personal development of each member. This has inspired the desire for an ongoing collaboration between colleagues with a view also to reinforcing the therapist's individual experience.

This book is intended therefore to share the findings of our journey so far, and the knowledge we have gained during the past years, in the hope that still unresolved thoughts and questions will inspire further engagement and exchange on both a clinical and a technical-theoretical level, with those who on a daily basis come across the same doubts and difficulties. We hope it will be useful in strengthening the basis from which we can build better relationships with our patients. We hope also to contribute to the ever more topical debate on how better to use psychoanalytic technique and theory in meeting the increasing demand for intervention with couples and families, and to delineate the unique value of psychoanalytic work in a territory that is still so little explored.

Theoretical background

The theoretical aspect of this volume highlights the relational aspects of psychoanalysis, alongside its intrapsychic dynamics, which together form the basis of a therapeutic approach to couples. The development of psychoanalytical theory within a model of the mind that envisions the acquiring of an identity and a sense of self, has given more relevance to understanding the personality in terms of its interaction with its significant emotional relationships. This is by contrast with the idea of developmental stages seen solely in relation to internal forces, as earlier envisaged in the structural model of urges and desires (Zavattini, 2008). With this in mind we have referred to concepts expressed by Melanie Klein (1963), Winnicott (1958), and Britton (1989). Winnicott was one of the first to emphasise the relational nature of human personality development and the significance from birth of the mother's specific and concrete care. He also stressed the importance of the adequacy of the mother's responsiveness to the baby's needs, for the child to develop continuity and integrity of being. Winnicott acknowledged that the real self of the child originates in and develops from the quality of this primary relationship. The development of the self is marked out by the growth of the affective sphere, which needs to be protected by the caregiver from the intrusion of inadequate environments. This is especially relevant to couple therapy given that each member of the couple is shifting between their individual goals and the desire to communicate and be understood within the relationship with the partner.

Britton reminds us of the importance not only of the mother's role but also of the relationship between the parents. The emotional environment they provide allows the child to engage in relationships where he is both observed by another (a third person, or two people) and also the external observer of a relationship between two people (the parents). If the relationship between the parents is founded on love, the child is helped to imagine a psychological space which is caring and accepting, and which is fundamental to secure and stable growth.

Many different approaches to psychological research have stemmed from such ideas, increasingly highlighting the importance of sharing, exchanging, and engaging in experiences with others, in order to develop adequately. This focus on relationships inspires the aim of enabling a mutual give-and-take with the partner. In optimal conditions the exchange allows self-regulation and reciprocal regulation, creating a balance that is flexible and dynamic (Beebe & Lachman, 2002).

In the realm of object relations theory, the mind is viewed as internalising not only objects but also relations and functions. Our understanding of the bond with the object and the ways in which this bond is sought has gained in complexity. Psychoanalytical research and theories originally concerned primarily with the individual, have developed this interest in the relational framework, focusing on how the individual interacts with other significant subjects (Bezoari & Ferro, 1991; Ruszczynski, 1993; Norsa & Zavattini, 1997; Fisher, 1999; Clulow, 2001, 2009; Manguzzi, 2010).

There are many references in this volume to the reconceptualisation of the idea of projective identification as both an intrapsychic and an interpersonal process. This allows light to be shed light on the shift of psychoanalytic approaches towards intersubjective interpretations of the couple relationship. It takes more than one person throughout the life of an individual to help him achieve 'unit status' in his psychological space (see Winnicott, 1958; Loewald, 1979; Gabbard & Ogden, 2009). In terms of the inner world, we see the connection with Bion's view of how the individual develops in the presence of a maternal mind that, especially in infancy, provides through a state of 'reverie' a thinking function in relation to its experienced emotions.

This volume refers to the concept of 'field' in two chapters: one in relation to theory, and another in relation to method. This concept was introduced by the Barangers (1961–1962) and was articulated in more depth in Bion's theories where, within the setting, it becomes a space between the patient and the therapist in which the relational dynamics between the characters of the story can take place. Many of psychoanalysis' concepts find expression in this area, oscillating between emotional movement and the construction of a new thought, a new story that is more adequate to the necessities of the relationship. Thus the search for concepts and theories that explain interpersonal dynamics, including those within adults, takes place in a scenario in which the relationship with the other is a necessary condition that persists throughout life (Norsa & Zavattini, 1997). The couple in this general sense can be seen as an essential core component of everyone's psychic life; and in our culture it is often considered (sometimes only implicitly) as a special, unique and original place that has its own identity alongside the individual identities of the partners, and that might therefore interfere with their personal aims and interests.

The research we present here aims to indicate hypotheses that embrace the many different psychopathologies we encounter in our studies and in real life. We would like to contribute to making sense of the disturbances that arise from the couple and family contexts and that have repercussions on a personal and a social level. Our approach is to concentrate on applying the specifics derived from individual psychoanalysis in a way that is feasible with couples and families. Working psychoanalytically, we are part of an ongoing process in which everything brought to the session needs to be welcomed and considered as potentially a source of development.

Last but not least, we would like to cite Thomas Ogden on how we may need help in making our experience dreamable and therefore thinkable:

> Beyond a certain point (a point that varies for each individual), we find it unbearable to think/dream our experience. Under such circumstances, if we are fortunate, there is another person (perhaps a mother or father, an analyst, a supervisor, a spouse, a sibling, a close friend) who is willing and able to engage with us in a process of dreaming our formerly undreamable experience.
> (Ogden, 2009, p. 113)

Every day in our work with couples it is our hope that this may happen.

Contents of the book

This book begins by considering how classical psychoanalytic theory has been developed into new models with methods that can welcome more than one individual personality into psychoanalytical territory: the couple, the family, the group. The first chapter, 'Psychoanalytic history and the couple relationship', reviews the psychoanalytic journey that has allowed its focus to extend from the mind of the individual to what happens when the minds of two individuals come into contact. Theoretical development has enabled the employment of some psychoanalytic tools in new therapeutic fields, such as the dynamics of couple relationships.

From the Kleinian school of thought onwards, psychic life has come to be seen as relational from its very beginning. The concept of projective identification opened up new ways of understanding how individuals enter into relation to the world and with that which is other than the self – extraneous, external, and a source of help but also of distress. The communicative function of this mechanism requires a responsive object (Campora & Zavattini, 2011). The many theoretical developments have taken different routes from this basic standpoint, using a variety of languages that are not always analogous. Nevertheless there are some points of contact in concepts such as Bion's container–contained, Bowlby's attachment and bonding, or Winnicott's 'holding' and environmental mother. In terms of clinical theory, we find that the listening role of the analyst fits well with the more recent relational viewpoints in which the therapy is seen not as a decoding process, but as a field in which the transformational experience can unfold (Kernberg, 2011).

In the second chapter, 'Theoretical foundations of psychoanalytic psychotherapy with couples', are described the theoretical concepts that have grown out of the formulations used in individual therapy and have been employed to construct the basis of couple psychotherapy. Links are made to show how the classic theories designed to describe the intrapsychic life of the individual merge into subsequent object relations theories that deal with psychic identity in terms of interpersonal relations (Dicks, 1967; Ruszcynski, 1995; Fisher, 1999). The concepts are noted which are most fruitful for working with couples, such as Bion's container–contained, communicative projective identification, and 'transformation'; and which can be used as a basis for identifying the contributions of both subject and object toward forming individual development. With regard to the concept of transformation, which has complicated implications in therapy, we make use of Ferro's (2002a, 2005) exposition of Bion's idea, which stresses not only the therapist's verbalisations but also the quality of his listening and the depth of his availability to the processes of psychic configuration taking place in the mind of the patient. The patient's transformative journey depends on all these factors. Indeed it has only become possible to work psychoanalytically with couples owing to this explicit acknowledgement of the total ensemble of influences that enable psychic distress to be reconsidered in its entirety. So in this chapter the dynamics of couple relationships, both functional and dysfunctional ones, are laid out, and some clinical examples are given for clarification.

In the third chapter, 'Equilaterality: the structure of the couple and the mental state of the therapist', the role of the therapist is highlighted together with his or her subjectivity and resonance on a countertransference level. In fact, dealing with the couple relation creates a situation in which none of the members of the relation (either the partners or the therapist) can be understood without the other since the dynamics emerging in the session depend on mutual interaction. The concept of relation itself implies the amplification of the psychic space, meaning that we are not dealing only with the individual's psychic space but also with the imaginary (not material) space in which the relationship takes place and where their internal worlds encounter each other and their emotions and objects intertwine. Owing to this the basic structures of the couple relationship are best represented by a triangle. Studying the transference–countertransference dynamics in a clinical case we recognise that the quality of triangularity can evolve, crystallise, and oscillate during the life cycle of a couple, assuming equilateral or scalene forms. The 'equilateral' function of the therapist is discussed in depth. This function describes how the relationship between the two partners is itself the patient. If a third party is present in an observational capacity, it is possible for projections to be withdrawn, leaving space for a more satisfying relationship. A triangular space has been created in which each partner can reflect on their own needs, on the needs of the other, and on the requirements of their relationship.

The fourth chapter, 'The therapist at work: technical matters', describes the methodology of psychoanalytic treatment of the couple, with reference to the theoretical models mentioned above. The joint setting is a space in which the actual partners, the imaginary partners that exist in one another's minds, and the relationship itself, are all present. In this chapter the transference and countertransference movements and the different levels of intervention carried out by the therapist are discussed through clinical examples. The shift is highlighted from 'reconstructive' models of the mind to those that emphasise the possibilities of change sparked off by new experiences. As a consequence it is clear how interpretation (in the classical sense) is only one aspect of our work, which mostly focuses on the emotional atmosphere and the psychic dynamics that emerge during the session itself.

In order to keep in context the implications of different psychoanalytical approaches, and to enrich the landscape of contributions through an ongoing exchange of ideas, the fifth chapter, 'The meeting of couple psychoanalysis with the inter-subjective viewpoint', explores the technical and theoretical basis of the relational intersubjective approach to couple ther-apy. This model asserts the need to increase the relationship's ability to contain, support and adjust the disturbing elements. The accent is on the ability to regulate emotion, meaning the proximity–distance tension between the partners, with the aim of improving its transformative potential. Through interpreta-tion, the quality of connectivity and attunement with the other is highlighted. The aim, both implicit and explicit, is therefore to find methods of regulating feelings. The therapist's function is to become involved in the intersubjective relation, available through his engagement to offer a new, alternative experience which can be memorised by the patient. The patient is given the opportunity to explore the subjectivity of the therapist and to improve their ability to recognise the other's mental state, intentions and emotions. They can then apply this experience to the situation with their partner, and the therapeutic transformation consists in this improvement in empathic understanding.

Finally, we would like to thank Professor Giulio Cesare Zavattini, for his availability and generosity in sharing his wealth of experience and knowledge and in supervising the coming-together of this book. And we dedicate this book to all our couples and patients.

Barbara Bianchini, Marina Capello, Laura Dallanegra,
Maria Adelaide Lupinacci, Fabio Monguzzi, and Lidia Vitalini

CHAPTER ONE

Psychoanalytic history and the couple relationship

Laura Dallanegra

It requires two minds to think one's most disturbing thoughts.
(Thomas Ogden, 2009, p. 100)

In order to illustrate our approach to this work, before we discuss the couple relationship as such, we would like to reflect on the historical development of psychoanalytic thinking and some of the rich, complex, and diverse contributions that are relevant to our theme. The aim of this first chapter is to highlight concepts that, though they may come from different theoretical perspectives, offer us useful tools for understanding the complex dynamics within the couple relationship. As when we visit an unfamiliar city, we can find our way with the help of a map, so in the same way, thanks to the advance of psychoanalytical thinking, we now have enough tools to undertake the exploration of new avenues. The dialogue that psychoanalysis has maintained with philosophical and scientific thinking has influenced its development on both a clinical and theoretical level. The constructivist epistemological approach, for example, has questioned the possibility of objective scientific knowledge in the sense of the representation of an external order independent of the observer. Even the observation of phenomena is considered an unreliable source for objective understanding, and has to take the observer into account.

Philosophical theories of knowledge dependent on a notion of scientific realism have by now faded, and theories maintaining that the subject plays an active role in construing its view of 'reality' are now dominant. Yet our subjective understanding is continuously adjusted through encounters with external reality. In psychoanalysis, we are now most interested in discovering what is happening in the relationship between two minds, rather than in the mind of the patient alone or believing that the analyst's information is objective. Various authors, from different schools of thought, have coined new terms to express the process whereby the analyst actively engages with the mind of the patient (see Bordi, 1995). Concepts such as 'holding' (Winnicott, 1961), 'role-responsiveness' (Sandler, 1976), 'enactment' (Filippini and Ponsi, 1993), 'intersubjective third' (Ogden, 1994), describe the contemporary view of the therapist, who is these days recognised as being an active participator in therapeutic change.

The matter of the relationship between the individual's psychic organisation and his external relational sphere is fundamental to the psychoanalytical debate, encouraging comparisons between different theories and opening up clinical experience to new avenues of intervention. In some cases the subject is not treated individually but in relation to a parent, a partner, a group. The relationship 'I–world, I–you' has been fundamental to the psychoanalytic panorama ever since the development of object relations theory, highlighting the profound influence of early emotional relationships in shaping personality structure. This has expanded the horizon of knowledge by clarifying the limitations of focusing solely on an individual mind when hoping to sufficiently understand a personality.

Internal world and external reality

Within the couple relationship, internal world and external reality intertwine in a particularly complex way. From its very outset psychoanalysis has looked at the relationship between internal and external realities with great interest, allowing within its clinical circumference a glimpse in the direction of the individual's other relationships. Some good examples are therapy with children or adolescents and their parents; group analysis; and most recently, the interest in the couple relationship. The following brief survey of the direction psychoanalytical research has taken is inevitably limited in scope, but necessary for our project.

Psychoanalysis' initial interest in the mind as a home for impulses, denial, and the unconscious, has evolved into the investigation of internal relational dynamics. In 1921 Freud described the individual mind's potential to either reach out or to close itself to the other: 'In the individual's mental life someone else is invariably involved, as a model, as an object, as a helper, as an opponent; and so from the very first individual psychology, in this extended but entirely justifiable sense of the words, is at the same time social psychology as well' (p. 69). All these relations are to be distinguished from the narcissistic 'satisfaction of the instincts' in which the personality is withdrawn from communication with others.

The way in which individuals deal with the relationship between exterior and interior has been at the heart of psychoanalytical inquiry (Velotti & Zavattini, 2008). Both internal and external reality can be sources of either support or disturbance for the individual. Freud's first model saw the individual's past traumas as being unearthed from the unconscious and thereby relieved. 'Trauma' implies an excessive influx of excitement arising from an event whose impact was such that the individual was not able to process it adequately, resulting in psychopathology. Freud's second (structural) model considered how the elements that compose the psychic apparatus function, and outlined how the ego mediates between the id and the external world (Mangini, 2003). The mechanisms of introjection and projection provide the foundation for articulating the link between subject (internal organisation) and external reality:

> Under conditions whose nature has not yet been sufficiently established, internal perceptions of emotional and thought processes can be projected outwards in the same way as sense perceptions; they are thus employed for building up the external world, though they should by rights remain part of the internal world. (Freud, 1913, p. 64)

Although projection could also be involved in seeking relief from conflict, defence was not its original purpose. Freud's description of the core concept of projection led to Klein's slightly different formulation of projective identification. Klein developed Freud's idea about the transforming power of internal perception in terms of how a child's developing personality is shaped by projecting externally frightening figures and introjecting positive figures. Her theory, although originating in Freud's energy model, clearly departs from it. By contrast with the Freudian model where the object is just an endpoint for impulses, Klein's intuitions enabled the assignation of a more relevant role to the object. Through projective identification, the person could not only modify internal reality but also modify the reality of the other, who is invested with a need to think and respond accordingly. Both self and object construct themselves on the basis of continuous processes of projection and introjection.

For Klein, projective identification was essentially an intra-psychic phenomenon, although her phrasing does suggest an interpersonal interpretation of this mechanism: 'Identification by projection implies a combination of splitting off parts of the self and projecting them on to (or rather into) another person. These processes have many ramifications and fundamentally influence object relations' (Klein, 1955, p. 143). For Klein, the main role is always that of the internal world; emotional experiences, love and hate, are at the heart of human motivation. Although she focuses on the mechanisms employed by the individual to filter the external world, her concept of projective identification opened new perspectives onto the relation between self and external object. The 'depressive position' acknowledges the ambivalent emotions aroused by an object which is external and independent of the self.

In recent years Britton, reconsidering Klein's thinking, has described the child's acknowledgment and acceptance of the relationship between its parents in terms of a 'triangular space' that enables three types of experience: namely belonging to a relationship, being observed in a relationship, and observing the relationship between two people. He writes: 'The capacity to envisage a benign parental relationship influences the development of a space outside the self capable of being observed and thought about, which provides the basis for a belief in a secure and stable world' (Britton, 1989, p. 87).

One of the most significant movements in the development of psychoanalytical thinking is the shift from the idea of a unified mind, imagined like a written text although not easily interpretable, to the idea of a mind that develops owing to the nourishment and care of another mind – a relationship. Therapy is an encounter between two minds in which the analytic process makes the previously unconceivable, conceivable.

The significance of relationships

In Klein's model, projective identification cannot exist in relation to nothingness: the presence of an object is necessary in order to project. It is Bion, however, who points out explicitly that this mechanism has not only a defensive but also a communicative function. This communicative function is based on the presence of a containing maternal mind equipped with a capacity for reverie and receptive to the child's projection (Bion, 1959). Reverie allows the projection to enter the mind of the object, which responds actively, comprehending and containing. The object of projection is not indifferent but on the contrary, functions by metabolising emotional 'elements' through 'alpha-function'. This allows for greater articulation of the relationship between subject and object, introducing what has been called the 'principle of circularity' (Velotti & Zavattini, 2008). Grotstein (1981) explains that this model of projection and containment forms the basis of normal thinking and is usually internalised by the child.

Different conceptual models arise from this, leading to different ways of perceiving the psychoanalytical process. For the sake of simplicity we can say that one model is based on the concept of instinct, another model on the concept of relationship. The first model aims to bring to consciousness the pathogenic intrapsychic conflicts by reconstructing the patient's experiences; the second creates a dyadic analytical situation. What emerges in the consulting room is the product of the interaction between therapist and patient (Jiménez, 2006). On the other hand the classic concepts of transference and countertransference, projective identification, object relations theory, introjection and projection, the Oedipus complex, and the formation of the superego, are foundational also to a relational outlook. Indeed many different post-Freudian approaches, in a variety of languages and settings, use the idea of 'relational'. As Jiménez writes: 'It is not an exaggeration to say that, each time clinicians with different psychoanalytical cultures try to communicate with one another, the "Babelisation" of psychoanalysis is reproduced' (2006, p. 146). While in the classical Freudian view the analysis aims to uncover historical events in the patient's life, in the Kleinian, the therapist's task is to aid the patient to deal with the internal ghosts by interpreting and analysing the defences surrounding separation and projection.

In Bion's model, the analyst–patient relationship takes precedence. In his theory of infant development, and consequently of the psychic processes of the individual mind, all new experiences are disturbing. At birth the infant is overwhelmed by new sensations deriving from both interior and exterior reality, which then generate 'beta-elements', being 'sense-impressions linked to an emotional experience' (Bion, 1962, p. 17). In this initial phase of life such overpowering stimuli can only be evacuated through projective identification until another mind transforms them into thoughts (symbols, dream-thoughts) by means of alpha-function. Bion's model does not focus on denial, splitting, or traumatic events that have taken place in the past or that are unconsciously phantasised; instead it emphasises the specific and characteristic ability of human beings to 'think thoughts, feel emotions, dream dreams' (Ferro & Vender, 2010). This ability forms and develops through the relationship between two minds and through the primitive, unconscious channel of communication which is projective identification. As with alpha-function, Bion's concept of the container-contained relationship is fundamental to the development of a theory of couple analysis. Elements of emotional experiences, arousing anxiety and requiring containment, are shaped within the container into dreams and thoughts. In favourable conditions, the relationship between container and contained enables growth of both aspects: the ability to carry out unconscious thinking expands and the thoughts are deepened and enriched. Pathology results when this psychic relationship fails. This relationship – the process of thinking – develops in order to digest disturbing emotional elements, and the interaction between thoughts and thinking persists throughout the individual's life. In a clinical situation, the aim is to help the patient to observe his own emotions and to develop his own capacity to think, through working with another mind in a process of continuing projection and introjection.

Since every stage in our development involves confronting new emotional experiences for which we are unprepared, we never lose this need to involve ourselves intimately with people with whom we can engage in thinking. Ogden writes: 'The two minds engaged in thinking may be those of the mother and infant, the group leader and group member, the patient and analyst, the supervisor and supervisee, the husband and wife, and so on' (2009, p.100). Bion's view of the mother–infant couple as container–contained has analogies with Winnicott's assertion (1961) that there is no such thing as a baby, only a baby and mother. Although coming from a different theoretical standpoint, Winnicott emphasises the need for a facilitating human environment – in the first instance the mother; the mother's ability to put herself in the child's place and understand its needs protects the child from the unthinkable fear of 'falling to pieces'. Whilst agreeing in part with Klein on object relations, Winnicott differs in his view that it is the quality of the environmental object that determines the self's development; this is something that also appears to connect with Bion's emphasis on maternal reverie as a service for processing the baby's emotional experiences.

Winnicott bases his view of the development of human personality entirely on relational grounds. He sees the essence of the child's developmental experience as its dependence on the supportive 'holding' environment provided by the mother. This is a natural function in the 'ordinary' mother whose 'primary maternal preoccupation' is based on empathy and does not require analytical reasoning. Yet although the baby is entirely dependent on his mother he can nevertheless be 'alone' in her presence (Winnicott, 1957, p. 418), and this is the nucleus of his true self and provides 'continuity of being' against a background of constant threat from what seems an intrusive and unsatisfying environment. He maintains that the self's ability to be alone is one of the most important indications of emotional maturity, and is the result of initial 'good enough' maternal care. He writes that 'The capacity to be alone is either a highly sophisticated phenomenon, one that may arrive in a person's development after the establishment of three-body relationships, or else it is a phenomenon of early life which deserves special study because it is the foundation on which sophisticated aloneness is built' (1957, p. 416). So for Winnicott there exists a paradox between the need of the true self to remain concealed and isolated for its own preservation, and the desire and necessity of every individual to communicate and be understood within a relationship.

We believe that Winnicott's idea of the self needing another distinct and separate self in order to fully exist, even when at the same time feeling threatened by anxiety about intrusion or a lack of correspondence in the other, is an appropriate nexus for examining the problems that arise in couple relationships. A facilitating environment should allow each partner to be alone in the presence of the other. We will investigate this in the following chapters.

The contribution of relational theories

Current psychoanalytical thinking, although influenced by different approaches, imagines there to be a continuous fluctuation between the intrapsychic and inter-psychic dimensions (Bolognini, 2004). The focus has shifted from the belief that psychic reality evolves in successive predetermined stages to the idea that it continuously reorganises itself on the basis of what is registered and experienced by the subject. This includes the continuous interaction with other minds. The encounter with the other (which may also be another part of the self) gives rise to a third, mutually constructed element. In the clinical setting, the focus is on what happens in the 'here and now' of the analytic encounter, rather than on research and reconstruction of the patient's past. The analysis becomes about finding a 'narrative truth' rather than an objective truth, picturing how the patient organises his or her experiences. This brings us closer to an 'authentic subjectivity in which a fluid identity is able accept unpredictability and cope with uncertainty' (Bordi, 1996, p. 24).

For a long time the dialogue between theorists, therapists and researchers was limited by the belief that their methods were antithetical. Their working environments were certainly a main point of difference: 'As practitioners we deal in complexity; as scientists we strive to simplify' (Bowlby, 1979, p. 5). Infant research has demonstrated that the child is biologically equipped to establish an active interaction with the surrounding environment, discovering patterns and thereby establishing expectations (Emde, 1988). As has often been observed, children discover very quickly the correlation between their activities and their mother's immediate reaction, resulting in a sense of effectiveness. The interpersonal relations of infancy are the foundation for relational psychoanalytic theories (Stern, 1985; Kernberg, 2011). Mother and child observation and research underlies the development of evolutionary theories such as attachment theory, highlighting the continuous process of co-regulation carried out by the child and caregiver in tandem. All of these conclusions boosted the general definition of intersubjectivity as something that enables a capacity to emphasise and resonate with someone else's experience. Each partner in a dyad (mother–child, analyst–patient, etc) can only be fully depicted in relation to the other. Self-regulation and interactive regulation are mutual and simultaneous processes that in ideal conditions exist in flexible and dynamic equilibrium (Beebe & Lachmann, 2002).

Bowlby was one of the first commentators to elaborate on how the quality of a primary attachment in early years is fundamental to the individual's development. His findings strengthened the bond between psychoanalysis and empirical research. According to Bowlby (1969–1982), a sense of trust built up by experience with the early caregiver can then be extended to other relationships; but if this fails, the object can become a source of fear and insecurity rather than of protection and reassurance. Although during infancy the attachment of child-adult is asymmetric, in adulthood attachment should manifest itself at a mutual level. When Bowlby refers to a 'sense of security' in the children observed, he means that they show they can admit dependence on the parents, but at the same time, that they feel themselves to be an independent entity. Relationships indicating distance, unresponsiveness, anxiety and ambivalence are insecure attachments. Insecurity, in this view, is not a personality trait but a feature of the particular relationship, and can vary according to circumstance.

Further evidence suggested it was not just the early years' experience as such, but the mental representations of it, that were significant in defining adult interpersonal relations. Internal working models are established on the basis of the reiterated experiences shared by the baby and the attachment figure, and are subsequently generalised. These are mental structures, configurations of the world that can be modified throughout life. They enable the person to plan, make decisions, interpret, anticipate, and thus to react appropriately to situations.

It is well known that Bowlby hypothesised that internal working models constructed in early life influenced the future success of a couple relationship. The difference of course is that in the adult couple each partner becomes an attachment figure for the other, trying to cope with the anxieties of being both dependent and an object of dependence (Fisher & Crandell,

2001). Ideally the fluctuation of inter-dependence in the course of responding to life's demands (childbirth, mourning, illness, work issues, etc) secures the smooth functionality of the relationship. Representational models that have proved to be secure in childhood enable the adult attachment relationship to be flexible, while an insecure childhood provokes rigid responses.

These ideas have influenced more recent formulations such as Fonagy's that the essential role of interpersonal experiences is to enable the individual to 'mentalise' (cited in Velotti & Zavattini, 2008). This entails an ability to regulate one's own emotional state in association with that of the other. It is a mechanism by which the child adjusts their emotional state in response to the caregiver's reactions, a sort of circular reflective process, named by Fonagy the 'reflective function'. It does not belong to the cognitive sphere but mainly to relational skills acquired through reoccurrence and an awareness of time – past, present, future – that enable the person to interpret their own experience and that which exists beyond themselves. Clearly the reflective function is necessary for the harmonious development of the individual in relation to the external world.

In recent years, the topic of intersubjectivity has become prominent in many branches of psychoanalysis, with a wide spectrum of theories (Zaccagnini et al., 2008). The 'intersubjective matrix' (Stern, 2004) denotes a process in which the mechanisms for identifying the mental states (intentions and emotions) of the other are innate. From early on the child is richly supplied with a variety of mental states that are accessible and recognisable as similar to the mental state of the other, and can be shared within the relational exchange. One intersubjective approach believes that the early imitational and emotional interactions are the result of human biological adaptation towards empathising with other fellow human beings; experience and maturation refine the individual's capacity for awareness of the other's emotional state. Fonagy and others (2002), however, insist the infant is biologically orientated towards the external world and its exploration, and the parents' empathic reflection evokes an imitative response in the baby; the term coined for this is 'objective intersubjectivity'.

Stern (1985), who has greatly informed this field, developed his thinking from a dual standpoint: evolutionary research and child development on the one hand, and psychoanalysis on the other. Observation demonstrates how from early on the infant has the capacity to interact with the real world and to establish social relationships with other human beings. As with psychoanalysis, research shifts its focus from the child to the relationship between mother and child. Stern's model is one of continuous development in the face of interaction between the individual and the environment. He observed that this does not refer necessarily to events as such, but rather, to our 'psychic reconstruction of what has happened' (1995, p. 83). These successive subjective experiences form the basis for the organisational principles of development. Stern believes the stages of development are not fixed, but are different ways of experiencing the social life of the self, and therefore it is not possible to undergo a regression in the traditional sense. He uses the term 'reflective conscience' to denote that which derives from interaction with the other; and intersubjective motivation arises from the need to work out 'where we stand' and 'what is going on' (Stern, 2005, p. 133). This monitoring is continuously updated during the dyadic encounter. Stern defines as 'intersubjective desire' one of the reasons for which therapy may be sought – that is, the patient's desire to be known and to find mental intimacy. 'Intersubjective consciousness' is the reflective form through which we can become conscious of our mental contents once they are handed back to us by the other.

The above-mentioned theories are some of those that have arisen from infant research and have had a strong influence on the clinical field. The focus on the intersubjective exchange supports the 'here and now' of the psychoanalytic encounter and the search for new creative pathways; and also, gives space for the emergence of a nonverbal emotional narrative, owing to its emphasis on intuitive sharing and emotional attunement.

I will conclude this section with a reference to the theoretical model developed in the last twenty years by the American relational psychoanalysts (Mitchell & Aron, 1999; Bromberg, 1993, 1998; Stern, 1985, 1989), and that links the idea of a continuous relations–dialogue with that of a non-unified self. In particular Bromberg, following Sullivan (1940, 1953), has a vision of the psyche as something which is not necessarily fragmented by pathological processes, but rather has never been unified; its sense of identity derives from a multiplicity of partial self–other configurations that are continuously negotiating with one another. From this perspective, the intrapsychic and the interpsychic realms (internal and external realities) can penetrate one another. This is relevant to working with couples as it envisions the need to seek for an equilibrium between personal feelings (the existing self) and the search to build new meanings, to achieve the stance that Sullivan defined as good interpersonal adaptation. Here again the goal of psychoanalysis is not to reconstruct the patient's past to achieve an insight into it, but to construct new connections between the many aspects of the self and internal and external reality.

The concept of field

In the relational models of psychoanalysis, as we have seen, the analyst is seen as a co-author rather than spectator of the change happening within the analytic relationship. As the Barangers put it: 'Each unit of the couple is unreadable without the other' (Baranger & Baranger, 1961–1962, p. 27). The 'field' concept introduced by them is inspired by Merleau-Ponty (1951), and describes neither individual but rather the situation in which the relationship is immersed. This becomes a third element with independent qualities and dynamics and is defined by the time and space in which the session takes place. In the analytic field, both analyst and patient form bastions, pockets of resistance, that are overcome only by the analyst's 'second look' which provides a detached view of what is going on. The analyst, while contributing to the formation of the field, is considered also to be able to observe and interpret the functional or dysfunctional operations taking place.

The field theory suggests that the encounter between individuals creates a new psychic space; subject and object are not always distinct and may be reversible (Neri, 2007). In other words, as Ferro says (2007, 2009), the field concept amplifies the definition of 'relation' by extending its constituents to the analytical situation itself. From a clinical point of view this creates a link with Klein's projective identification and Bion's alpha-function, reverie, and container–contained, and with the recent ideas about narrative and how the transformative function of the analytical experience takes place.

In Bion's revision of the concept of projective identification, which is reflected in most current theoretical and clinical approaches, the mother's role in the child's development is crucial, since she is unconsciously capable of 'dreaming' the experiences that the child cannot cope with, making them available 'in a form that he is able to utilise in dreaming his own experience' (Ogden, 2004, p.1357). The container and contained describes a process, not simply the objects that are relating to one another. The content is continuously changing and expanding in response to undigested sense experiences (beta-elements). Projective identification, viewed in this way, becomes the universal communication channel that activates the function of the container and reverie. A failure of communication in either partner can result in development being blocked and a feeling of being surrounded by an external world which is unmoving and sterile.

Each member of a psychoanalytical relationship carries their own psychic field into the session, inhabited by all sorts of turbulences and intrapsychic possibilities; but when these are immersed in the setting, the mental mating between analyst and patient creates a third field, an intermediate space where characters and dramas map out a matrix of relational movements. The field includes the setting, the relationship operating through projective identification, the transference and countertransference. It has an oscillating nature, and is 'the place where all the potentialities and the worlds emerging from the relationship between analyst and patient can take place' (Ferro, 2007, p. 65). According to Bion (1962), in the case of patients whose alpha-function is deficient, it may be necessary to build the container before the disturbing content can be accessed and the story can be told. The workshop-mind is not automatic; the field can generate the development of the container.

In conclusion, we have tried to delineate how psychoanalysis has moved from its original exclusive interest in the intrapsychic world, in the direction of the relational or interpsychic worlds that are formed by the interaction between minds and their environments. The evolution of the individual is not seen as having a set pattern, but instead, the therapeutic interest is dedicated to the acquiring of tools and experiences 'that make the subject more equipped to encounter what is not yet known about the self and the other' (Ferruta, 2011). In working with couples, similarly, we do not wish to propose a series of problems and answers but rather to illustrate the complexity of the forces that are involved in this kind of work. To quote Bolognini:

> It is up to us to allow connections that appear unexpected or incoherent to co-exist, in a middle ground. Sometimes with patience these connections become less contradictory than was initially thought, just as in a family or group environment certain contributions may seem to undermine the coherence of the general attitude but eventually prove to be very fertile. (Bolognini, 2008, p. 22)

CHAPTER TWO

Theoretical foundations of psycho-analytic psychotherapy with couples

Barbara Bianchini and Lidia Vitalini

The problem is how to let the germ of an idea, or the germ of an interpretation, have a chance of developing.

(Wilfred Bion, 1985, p.12)

The previous chapter has shown that the theoretical developments behind the move from a reconstructional approach to an object relations approach in psychoanalysis are complex and diverse. The latter are based on the belief that the relation between object and subject regulates the emotional and developmental state of the individual. Thus the focus shifts to the quality and characteristics of the encounter with the other. From this perspective, the therapeutic task is an evolutionary journey of co-construction by therapist and patient, that utilises interpersonal relationships to link with the relationships of the patient's inner world.

The pioneers of psychoanalytical psychotherapy with couples began with their knowledge of the clinical methodology of individual psychoanalysis, and therefore used individual sessions as the setting for each member of the couple. The practice of undertaking joint sessions with both partners present came into being as a result of the increasing use of interpersonal approaches to psychoanalysis. The couple and the therapist all participate in the rhythm and cycle of the exchanges (Dicks, 1967; Fisher, 1999). This approach proved to lead to more satisfactory communication between all the participants, and also to a better understanding of the emotional experiences of the couple. A new field of research and a new theoretical and clinical debate took shape, at present still growing, owing to the gradual increase in demand for crisis therapy for both couples and families. In the course of this, joint sessions have become the favourite setting for couple therapy.

Couple therapy as it currently stands has been shaped by the work of its clinical pioneers (Pincus, 1960; Teruel, 1966; Dicks, 1967) and by the additional assimilation of contributions from other fields of research, such as developmental psychology and group psychotherapy, which have emphasised new theoretical ideas regarding ways of self-discovery and investigation. We will note some of these concepts and their use.

Individual development, the role of the other, and the discovery of the analytic third

We would like first to detail in more depth certain important aspects of personality development that are relevant to couple therapy, highlighting in particular the function of the 'other' in the development of the individual. Our theoretical framework is based on the development of object relations and the mechanisms of projection and projective identification. For the passage of emotions from within to outside the self, in order to cope with conflict and anxiety, determines and conditions all our relationships and is the primary mover in personality development. Hence the importance of the quality of the exchange with the caregiver within the emotional sphere, the feelings of love and hate which are foundational to human motivation. From birth, the child seeks to establish emotional links with an object and starts to make sense of experience as a result of the responsiveness and effectiveness of this dyadic relation.

Grotstein (1981) writes that the ability of the child's self to exist within the world relies on functions that contain, filter, dilute and diminish the intensity of his or her emotional experiences. Together with the establishing of this initial maternal bond, family life confronts the child with another transition: the discovery of the father. The mother–father–baby trio that marks out the child's developmental environment was denominated by Britton (1989) as a 'triangular space', in which the child has the opportunity to take part in the family relationship but also to observe the parents' relationship. The idea of a third place comes into being – a place in which the child can observe object relations. The acceptance of the existence of a special bond between the parents gives the child's psychic world coherence and promotes development. He is aware of the separate bonds with each parent and also of the union between them of which he is only witness not protagonist; he is both included and excluded; aware of different types of relationship and of generational boundaries.

The unconscious introjection of the parental figures as a couple (via the triangular configuration) underlies the child's ability to understand his mind and body during the major psychophysical changes of adolescence. Perceiving, though with ambivalence, the need for greater separation and exclusion from the parental couple, he or she will seek new types of emotional bonds with them in the course of trying to develop an individual identity.

Everyone agrees on the importance of working through the Oedipus complex, which goes with the relinquishment of phantasies of omnipotence, and is the emotional foundation for the experience of loss and separation needed to reach maturity. Nevertheless, working through the Oedipus complex does not necessarily mean that it is dealt with once and for all; the difficulties that derive from being part of a couple, and therefore the difficulties of a triangular situation, persist within the dynamics of adult life and can emerge with a substantial presence at certain points in life.

As an example we would like to present Carlo and Franca. We can see in the relational difficulties of the new couple how the unresolved ghosts of their past lives in their families of origin re-emerge.

Carlo is aged 40 and Franca is 30. It is the second relationship for each of them. During our first meetings they recounted
how they both came from disturbed family backgrounds marked
by intense grievances and illness. They both seemed in need of
finding a container figure in each other, that could offer stability
and security in the face of any external disruption. They met,
they fell in love, they had a child fairly quickly, so as to affirm the
good nature of their relationship. After the birth of their child,
they felt that all their time was taken up with their new parental
role and their main complaint was that they never had any time
for themselves.

Their relationship seems to be founded not on an adult object
partnership, but on an idealised phantasy that demands a type
of reciprocal fusion aimed at helping their own individual development. The container provided by falling in love had broken
down after the swift arrival of the third element – their child.
Carlo is very preoccupied with work, which is a source of stability and safety for him, and in his little free time he concentrates
on taking care of his child. Franca, who had been charmed by
Carlo's long and intense courtship, feels betrayed and abandoned,
lonely and frustrated. She continues to demand attention and
protection from her partner, she is unconsciously jealous of the
attention that they both give their child, and feels antagonistic
to the demands of everyday life, which has become for her a
fulltime prison that prevents her professional development.

A vicious circle has established itself, such that the greater
Franca's requirements and dissatisfactions, the more Carlo fears
for the child's adequate care, so he dedicates even more of his time
to the child and excludes his partner. So at present they are both
frustrated, distressed, and disappointed, and this has obscured any
feelings of tolerance and empathy towards each other.

The therapeutic exchanges brought out the existence of
intense, mutual and interlocking projective intrusions, based
not on the understanding of each other's existing needs, but
translated subconsciously into a belief in the other's power to
repair the past by building their own family: a new family which
would be proof of their victory over the past traumas caused
by their families of origin, and give them a legitimate sense of

personal adequacy and efficacy by showing they are better than their parents.

The intensity of this internal emotional propulsion has been so strong in each of them that at first it interfered with their undertaking a personal investigation into their own disturbance, their feeling of being unable to repair damage and to cope with frightening experiences. This personal responsibility had been unloaded onto the other in the expectation of a communal reparative process that would take shape in the form of their project of creating a family. The pre-eminence of these reciprocal needs, and the consequent anxiety and emotional fragility, seems to have induced the illusion they could bypass the necessary formative stages of the couple relationship, and to have made the concrete realities of everyday family life a focus for their fear of losing their own identity.

The mind of the therapist provides an opportunity to create a space for thinking and understanding the self that has not yet found a place within their relationship, and the therapeutic function consists in the opportunity to experience an object that is able to take care of them adequately.

We can summarise that the sense of being a couple, and the presence and employment of the third figure, relate both to the processing of the Oedipus complex and to a type of mating that satisfies the needs of both minds involved, as Bion has said. There is a constructive encounter between the person's developmental requirements and a facilitating environment, and the reciprocal exchange produces growth. In a healthy context, this is a process that continues from the early primal relationship of the dyadic/triadic exchange. The exchange needs to support awareness, identity and continuity in the sense of self, but also the possibility of being dependent in the sense of trusting in the relationship with the other.

Why together?

The 1970 reform of the divorce laws in Italy were part of a new socio-cultural environment which helped to make couple therapy possible. The atmosphere allowed for more awareness of the difficulties that may exist within couples, and therefore more freedom in expressing and attempting to resolve these difficulties; hence the demand for joint couple therapy has soared. A 'sick' relationship may be improved if difficulties can be faced and acknowledged; or if necessary, it can be guided through the process of separation in less conflictual and destructive ways. Being together is not an inevitable fixed condition, and blood ties are less paramount in families and parenthood. The reality of today's nuclear families includes a social network and affective bonds with people outside the family – neighbours, friends, parents of children's friends – often for logistical reasons, since they are living the same lifestyle and can concretely share help and support. The question of personal wellbeing therefore arises more easily, with each partner able to ask themselves: 'Would I be better on my own? With someone else?'

In the process of questioning why there is such a high demand for couple therapy we find that the distress is generally a communal one, projected onto the relationship itself, in the form of 'not feeling happy together'. The relationship tends to define itself in two-dimensional terms of 'I–him' and 'I–her' that flatten it to a series of purely functional exchanges serving to maintain a status quo. Therapeutic help is sought when reciprocal communication has failed and when it is not possible to cultivate a 'third function', so the analyst becomes the third figure, arbitrator of the disputes. We have described this function in terms of a stage in the child's development (Britton, 1989). If it is not fulfilled within the couple relationship itself, the therapist can serve a similar function, by offering a thinking viewpoint on the dynamics of the relationship.

This meant that requesting individual help was less constructive and it became requisite to bring the partner to join the analyst-stranger in trying to find a way out of the impasse. Often the partners come to therapy in the belief that the other is in the wrong and the source of their personal distress, hoping that if the other can change, the relationship can be repaired. This insistence on the need for the other to change expresses implicitly a lack of volition to change themselves. What also appears, even if subconsciously, is the search for absolution from one's own responsibilities. Often the awareness of a mutual responsibility is not present in the request for help, nor is the ability to reflect on communal problems, or to imagine the different possibilities that might exist within each partner's role and that might help to improve the existing situation. The analyst needs to become the analyst of both individuals in order to fulfil impartially and equidistantly the missing role of the 'third'.

In answer to the question of why they ask for joint help, Fisher says that in the couple situation, the splitting can exist either between the partners (within the couple) or internally (within each partner): 'The difference with a couple is that the splitting can be between the partners as well as internal to them – the splitting between the self who will under no circumstances seek out a therapist, and the self who is desperate for help' (Fisher, 1999, p. 209). Fisher differentiates between elements belonging to the self and elements of internal objects. Both types can be intrusively split and projected toward the other (p. 142). Some of these projective movements can concern both self (such as emotions) and the self's internal objects (such as, a loved object) (p. 119). This is why we welcome proposals for joint couple therapies, considering how difficult, in fact impossible, it is to separate these various elements at the beginning.

As in individual therapy, the therapist plays a parental role, creating a harmonious and safe relationship with each partner such that they feel understood first as individual people and then as a couple. 'Being understood' is often given as the most important factor in coming to therapy. Ambivalent feelings are often brought when there is a request for joint therapy: on the one hand a wish for change is expressed; on the other, a demand is evident for the display of defensive emotions. What seems most desired is to legitimise the reason for their emotional state – to hand the patient a 'receipt' (Ferro, 2009). Feeling personally understood helps in understanding the other, and in developing a new bond.

The joint session model and 'unconscious fit'

The middle of the last century in London saw many developments in the psychoanalytical field, including Bion's work on group psychotherapy, from which was derived the definition of a setting suitable for couple psychotherapy. In 1949, working under the auspices of the Tavistock Clinic, Henry Dicks selected a number of couples for psychotherapy and studied them with a view to understanding how to help alleviate marital distress. He tried to understand the significance of unconscious communication, the quality of the bonding, and the characteristics of the emotional involvement. Dicks chose a methodology that focused on the investigation of 'internal worlds shared in common' by the partners. Initially, believing in the need to establish a safe relationship between patient and therapist, Dicks devised a method where each patient underwent individual sessions with their own therapist, followed by discussion between the therapists. Before long however he decided to take on joint sessions in order to achieve a better understanding of what each spouse meant when they referred to one other. This method meant it was possible to address the conflicts deriving from the socio-cultural roles of each partner, their personalities, and the unconscious intertwining of their developmental and emotional stories.

In joint sessions we witness the internal relational dynamics of each patient, and at the same time the unfolding of the couple relationship; then with the addition of the therapist we see the symbolic representations of the triangular exchange. The complexities that emerge from this encounter legitimise the relevance of joint therapy for couples. In *Marital Tensions*, published in 1967, Dicks referred to object relations theory and defined the significant affective relationships as 'neutral therapeutic relations'. He used concepts derived from Klein, such as projective identification and splitting, in order to suggest that the partner becomes the 'holder' of the other's projected and split features. Furthermore he highlighted the multiform structure of the couple relationship and formulated concepts such as 'unconscious fit' and 'collusion'. Unconscious fit is the third dimension resulting from two adjoining independent worlds. It indicates finding an emotional reciprocity in which the boundaries of the individual ego fade. Collusion is the term used to describe the unconscious defence mechanism which maintains an equilibrium in which intolerable features of each partner's self are inseparable from the functioning of the relationship itself.

In the beginning psychoanalytic psychotherapy was based on reconstructive logic: trying to understand how, within their personal history, each party's organisation interwove with the other; and within the history of the couple, what led to their choice and why they have stayed together. Later however, in line with the psychoanalytic model of the 'here and now' and the view that psychic life is a continuous scanning of the mental states of the self and the other (Beebe & Lachmann, 2002), couple therapy came to focus on the live process of the third dimension produced by the encounter between the two people. Unconscious fit refers to the mutual flux of identifications continuously taking place in the present. The relationship is the expression of many variables based on the individual and mutual regulation of these identifications. In addition to unconscious fit, the most recent developments of the 'field' theory (as mentioned in the last chapter) are also useful in understanding the complexity of the unconscious functioning during the session: these include not only the internal worlds of each partner and their interrelation but also the mind of the analyst, his reverie, internal objects, and countertransference.

Dicks noted that a shared ego-boundary is formed by the unconscious bonds of the couple unit; he called this a 'dyadic membrane', a kind of skin enveloping and protecting the relationship from intrusions from the external world. The quality of this membrane and the forms that it takes inform the therapist about the functioning of the conjugal relationship. When it is sufficiently flexible and permeable to external influx, the dyadic membrane can be a tool for intimacy and the protection of privacy, and it contributes to the growth and enrichment of the relationship. The dyadic membrane may become too porous, so ineffective in filtering out the external intrusions that jeopardise the necessary 'sense of us' (G. S. Klein, 1976) that is fundamental for the couple's functioning. On the other hand, the membrane may also become so rigid that it completely excludes the external world, resulting in a dyadic fusion with a shared and undifferentiated self (Giannakoulas, 1992). The definition of the concept of projective identification given by Ogden (1979) is useful in this context for understanding the reciprocal identifications present in the couple. It affirms projective identification to be something that really takes place between two people who are closely linked, not just the omnipotent phantasy of an individual. Ogden summarises this psychological process as, simultaneously, a method of defence, a way of communicating, a primitive form of object relation, and a journey of psychological change in which difficult feelings may be handed to the other and thus become 'available for a new internalisation' (Caporali, 2010, p. 847).

Dicks also depicts the strong conflicts and reciprocal frustration present in many couples when they use the relationship as a means of creating their own wished-for world of object relations. The need to idealise or denigrate parts of the self or of the other often originates in the attempt to avoid the sense of confusion produced by the ambivalent feelings of love and hate which are always part of a relationship.

Unconscious fit is not therefore the sum of two partners' individual characteristics but an entity in itself. Dicks focuses interest on the transference between the partners and suggests that re-balancing defence mechanisms such as projective identification and idealisation play their part in the process of choosing the partner. Projective identification attributes to the other unwanted parts of the self, unrecognised expectations, and illusions linked to the idealised roles often assigned to internal parents. Choice of partner is precise, not casual; the other has to prove themselves an adequate container of uncomfortable feelings and also custodian of that which needs to be protected.

Romantic love and infantile identifications

Developing these points further, in the light of psychoanalytic thinking since Bion, we can say that we choose our partner as if in a dream, assigning him or her the role of a character that suits our own desire, and when this is reciprocated we become fascinated as if by a magic spell (Dallanegra, 2007). The unconscious creates a phantasy or dream involving the other person, the stranger, giving one another leading roles in the way that a director casts a play. Our minds are full of characters and actors, but they are not full of authors: we are the one and only author. It becomes very difficult for us to change the narrative. The story becomes repetitive, static, always the same; if the actors never become tired of their role, they will continue to live the same narrative, the same conflicts and the same stresses. Then sometimes, as the actors become tired of their given roles, we may wish to redistribute the roles or find others to play them. However if one is lucky, the person who is prepared to grow and 'learn from experience' (in Bion's sense) may find his or her actors helpful in the playing out of new narratives.

The phenomenon of romantic love is based on a dream of love and it is a transference phenomenon, that is, it is the externalisation of an internal object or situation. In order to shift from infantile transference (in touch with physiological needs) to adult transference (in touch with internal objects) it is necessary to relinquish omnipotent expectations of one's parents, by understanding that they could not do everything and didn't know everything, but that they did what they could, and not allowing this to dampen the love on both sides. In the same way, the elements of infantile transference that are part of the experience of falling in love inevitably cease following a process of disillusion, and may then be replaced by the adventurous process of learning to accept and understand one's own love object in depth.

When Dicks describes love relationships as 'natural therapeutical relationships' he means that they are a place where early unresolved object relations find expression: in particular, in the concept of 'holding partner', someone takes on the role of container of certain infantile aspects of the other partner's self that they have been assigned. Thus the concept of reciprocity is seen as essential in human relations. We use interpersonal relations as an opportunity to repair unresolved aspects of our object relations or to find new ways of adapting and developing them. Thus the linear model of psychological disturbance gives way to a reciprocal one in interpersonal relationships.

Couple therapy aims to help each partner regain their own lost (projected) features in order to promote the emotional maturity that will allow them to live in affective intimacy with another person. This will enable them not to hold grudges in the face of frustration but to tolerate ambivalent feelings and abandon the urge for revenge, and instead to achieve an attitude of respect towards the other partner and their individual identity. During the therapeutic process unresolved emotional crises in the development of each partner emerge together with the primitive defence mechanisms that attack the relationship. A couple may nonetheless continue to stay together even in a state of pain and conflict, in the hope that the part of their inner world entrusted to the other will still eventually find its primary regressive needs for object love satisfied.

We have to consider therefore whether the internal problems of one partner have found responsiveness in the internal world of the other, or whether they have entered into collusion.

Collusion

The concept of collusion was developed by Dicks to indicate the negative aspects of the relationship maintained between partners through the roles unconsciously assigned to one another. Collusion is an active process that occurs during the formation of the couple and it is the expression of the persistent involvement of previous unresolved object relations that block the developmental process and the achievement of adult maturity. Often both partners wait for an answer to their needs without even articulating a proper request to the other: thus what happens is that one partner starts to represent the potential and the functions that the other is lacking. The term 'collusion' derives from *ludere* (to play), but also from *illudere* (to deceive): collusion is, by nature, a shared illusion, a deception.

In this respect, Laing (1961) has noted how in the other person we not only seek a hook on which to hang all our projections, but we may also try to force him or her to embody the object we wish to complete some particular identification. He defines collusion as a march between two personalities on the basis of shared primitive anxieties and object needs. According to Losso and Packciarz: 'Collusion is the result of two infantile scenarios that reinforce each other and create a new scenario using current representations: a contemporary comedy with themes that belong to the past is re-enacted' (2000, p. 80).

In an interview with Fisher, Meltzer defines collusion as an alliance towards a shared aim that has to do only with survival; it is 'a political relation, characterised by grandiosity and absolutely egocentric' (Ruszczynski & Fisher, 1995). Norsa and Zavattini define collusion as a type of negative unconscious fit in which 'what emerges is a distorted interpretation of the partner's communication, one that highlights the negative aspects of the communication and of the feelings of the other person insofar as these represent the confirmation of expectations and negative convictions linked to internal relational contexts' (Norsa & Zavattini, 1997, p. 100). They continue:

> We can therefore define collusion as a defensive organisation built by two in which aspects of both partners that are split, perverse, superegoistic, are strengthened, creating an environment which is rigid, anti-libidinal, frustrating, but corresponds to the defensive necessities of each partner. (Norsa and Zavattini, 1997, p. 101)

In collusion, therefore, each partner makes some of the characteristics of the other partner their own and imprints on them rigid aspects deriving from parts of themselves or their internal object, parts which are despised or idealised. In this way neither of them recognise themselves as contributing to the state of distress that they consciously want to avoid, and they both blame each other.

Over time such an organisation within the couple tends to create rigid modalities of operation that inhibit other parts of the self or of the internal objects from expressing themselves. Thus collusion is a double defensive organisation that can be compared to other individual defence mechanisms (splitting, denial, idealisation) that protect against the anxiety of loss and separation, and leads toward the projection and evacuation of the unwanted aspects of one's own internal world (Norsa & Baldassarre, 2007). It also prevents the reintegration of split aspects deposited into the other. Collusion in couples thus has an adaptive function in relation to the complexity of adult life, entailing a loss of awareness of pain and the price to be paid. In using an enormous amount of energy just to maintain the status quo in the relationship it can also become an obstacle to each individual's potential development.

By contrast, intimacy between partners entails them each becoming a container for the other through reciprocal reverie. A bond develops that enables them to grow both as individuals and as a couple. According to Meltzer (in Ruszczynski & Fisher, 1995), intimacy differs from casual or contractual relationships; it derives from the appreciation, gratefulness, and understanding of being treated according to one's own needs and not according to one's external value.

We believe that in couple life there is a constant oscillation between an adult level of integration and enrichment, unconscious complementarity and intimacy, and an infantile level of idealisation, expectation, evacuation, and reciprocal tyranny. Both these possibilities form a continuum that modulates and changes with the varying requests with which the life cycle confronts the couple.

One of the therapeutic objectives of couple psychotherapy is de-collusion and differentiation so that each partner can become aware of their own unconscious motivations as re-enacted through the relationship. Enhancing the capacity to take care of the fragile aspects of one's own personality has positive repercussions on the capacity to take care of the other, in the recognition that they are different and separate from one's self. On the other hand the therapist can also try to make use of the important role that collusion plays in keeping partners together, but working through it in order to unravel its negative bonds.

Concrete and representational

Something that differentiates a joint session from individual therapy is the welcoming of each partner both as a real person and in their role as an internal object for the other person. A person who is concretely present, not just represented (as in individual therapy), requires an extension of our thinking; we are in the presence of the actual relationship itself. It is different also from a group setting in which the encounter is between strangers. Work with couples is complicated also by the fact that among many other roles, the therapist is also playing that of the outsider: the 'relational territory' of the couple precedes the analytical encounter, has an existence of its own, and returns to its routines outside the setting.

To return to the example of Carlo and Franca. The sessions with this couple have followed a repetitive pattern for a long time. In the initial stages Franca blamed Carlo for refusing to discuss things with her, always saying dismissively 'Lets talk about it on Thursday' (meaning during the session). Carlo blamed the little time that he has and his tiredness after a full day at work. Nevertheless it is not long before his need emerges for strong emotional control. He is afraid of exaggerating, exploding, and therefore being dangerous; he is afraid of hurting Franca if he expresses what he feels. It becomes clear that the continuous complaints and requests of Franca remind him of the pattern of his relationship with his mother, to whom he used to reply when annoyed by leaving the house and slamming the door.

For Carlo, the therapist becomes the concrete object: the outsider whose mediating function enables communication with his partner, creating a boundary safe from possible emotional excesses – his fears of communication degenerating into something uncontrolled and explosive. But Franca's evacuations also need to be received and contained by the therapist, who is careful to create a boundary for reciprocal projections and possible reassignments of personal responsibility.

The therapeutic function involves helping them to express their emotions, both the ones held back and the ones evacuated, modulating them, and translating them in the form of emotional states that are tolerable to them. The relational exchange will be less burdensome if a way can be found for the acknowledgement and gradual reappropriation of aspects that belong to the emotional nexus of each partner.

Fisher (1999) emphasises how a clinical situation such as this one can be very delicate and he points out how movements of pathological complicity between the partners become manifest, unconsciously designed to maintain cohesion between the couple and to exclude the 'outsider', who takes the form of both the analyst in person and of the relationship that emerges from the scenario of the setting. Fisher also points out that, although it is not possible to make a clear differentiation between couple therapy and individual therapy, it is the psychic reality of the relation between the therapist and the couple that forces all three to confront their imagination and their own intuition. During the session one should never dismiss the importance of two aspects: the fact that every relational movement happens in the presence of the other, whether phantasised and internal or real and external, so this nourishes feelings of being extraneous and excluded of which the analyst needs to be aware and take into account.

We believe that we need to make it part of our therapeutical competence to appreciate this concreteness, and interpret it into representational terms of the life of the couple. We need to build safety nets that can support feelings of emptiness within the couple and the inability to think about themselves, in order to find the specific qualities of each personality. This will help each partner to free themselves from the confusion of non-specific and undifferentiated attributes that have been produced by excessive projective identification, preventing a 'couple state of mind' from forming (Morgan, 2005).

Although we agree with the difficulty of differentiating the real object from the psychological representation, given the sense of reality that the external presence of a person brings, we believe that it is best to consider the meaning of behaviour in terms of internal functioning, unconscious phantasies and emotional states. As Bion affirms, it is the emotional experience of the intimate relationship that needs to be understood in order for the mind to develop. Ferro (2007) likewise emphasises the difficulty of confronting the intensity and quantity of emotions in mental structures which are never adequate enough to modulate those emotions. We need to be aware of the strategies that we use to hide and protect ourselves from the difficulties that emotional reality presents us with – our own, and in relation to that of the other. The interplay of intrapsychic and interpersonal movements means that the shared emotional experience becomes a temporary confused barrier where each partner is unable to recognise their individual sources of anxiety.

Relational territory of the couple – the setting

We would now like to introduce the notion of the 'relational territory of the couple'. By this we mean the territory constructed and inhabited throughout the relationship, a shared territory where the reality of the internal world and the reality of the external world intertwine. Here, in the transitional space of 'us' (Kaës, 2001), an intersubjective space supported by the realities of everyday life, the project of forming a relationship is planted by the couple and grows. The analyst is excluded from this territory but the couple return to it after each session. Kaës relates relational theory to the mental functioning of the couple in the double sense of group work and of unconscious basic assumptions, which brings us back to Bion's idea of group mentality (1961, 1970) in which the hope for a work group composed of individual risks being sabotaged owing to an uncontainable flux of proto-emotions. Ferro (2007) defines as proto-emotions the non-metabolised precursors of the emotions from which the self needs to be freed since they obstruct the minds.

Bion describes various forms of relationship, including healthy (symbiotic or commensal) ones which produce growth, and destructive 'parasitic' ones (1970, pp. 78, 95). When there is psychic disturbance in the relational territory of a couple, a pathological functioning can form even without their awareness and have repercussions for all involved. In seeking for equilibrium, couples oscillate between these two types of relationship – the growth-producing and the parasitic – and the relational territory is a place, imaginary but real at the same time, where life unfolds and where both healthy and pathological couple interactions occur (Rouchy, 1998). It can also happen that the couple, unable to manage itself on an emotional level, bonds in a project that is entirely concrete, relevant only to the practical functionality of everyday life. This leads to the creation of an exclusively operational relationship.

As an example of such a relationship, we refer to the case of Mr and Mrs F, a couple in their forties who have known each other since adolescence. They say that they have realised their goals: marriage, family, professional achievement. But now they are not happy together and are contemplating separation, and ask for help. For the first time they realise that what they thought they wanted to build together has not brought them happiness. Driven by their family project they operated solely on a concrete level, neglecting to listen to their emotional world; they just dedicated themselves to the project. Middle-age, for him, and the growing up of their children, for her, confront them with a sense of superfluity and loneliness. They realise that they haven't been bound by an emotional project based on accepting each other's needs and desires and therefore in continuous development. On the contrary, their bond took on definition more socially than personally, requiring only a prescriptive functioning without listening to emotions. They find that over time they have avoided confronting what they have unconsciously found upsetting and unsatisfying in each other, in the fear that this might get in the way of their stated programme and make them question whether they had got everything wrong.

This couple in effect asked the analyst to take on the role of judge in order to verify their failure and the impossibility of being happy together. They deemed it too late to reconsider their relationship at their age, and thought it best to end it and go their own ways. Their relational territory is one which has always paralysed any thinking about emotions and therefore stifled their development both as individuals and as a couple.

The recognition of the nature of the couple's relational territory, as it proceeds over time, is a necessary foundation for the work of revealing the unconscious and reciprocal emotional movements and the meanings that emerge. It is also necessary to be aware of how the demands of 'parasitic' bonds, lacking in thought, can become dominant in just one of the partners and have repercussions on the couple. They can also block the therapist's capacity for thought and the transformational possibilities of the field, resulting in an impasse in the therapy.

The relationship is the patient

As we have seen, the development of a theoretical model for couple therapy, with both intrapsychic and interpsychic elements, has been founded on Klein's concept of projective identification and Bion's of container–contained, which have been elaborated by many authors in this context (for example Ruszczynski, 1993, 1996; Fisher, 1999). We have seen how each partner can use the other to project undesired parts of the self, or to become a source of containment and development of the individual self (or even, both at the same time). This is why Ruszczynski (1996) asserts that 'the relationship is the patient', not simply the individual mind. In the couple relationship the 'marital triangle' can be thought of as created by both partners, with their relationship as the third element.

In couple therapy we are dealing with two individuals with distinct emotional worlds, but we also deal with the relation that the two individuals have created and that is in a state of disorder. During the joint session in the presence of both partners, the therapist embodies a parental role for the couple but also the role of third person, by entering into relation with the internal world of each partner. By creating a 'marital triangle' both partners have the opportunity to promote each other's psychological development; and it is in the triangular space that observation and containment can take place in order to reflect and formulate thoughts.

As Bion said (1959), the containment process is a function of the relationship, not just of one person or the other. The couple relationship has been envisioned by Colman (1993) as a container with both a spatial and temporal dimension; it is about the experience of being contained by the relationship during a process that evolves through time:

> *The relationship itself* becomes the container, the creative outcome of the couple's union, to which both partners can relate. It is an image of something the couple are continually in the process of creating, sustaining, and maintaining, while at the same time feeling that they exist within it – are contained by it. (Colman, 1993, p. 89)

The containing function needs to be able to absorb the tension born from the need to develop both inside and outside the relationship; being totally contained within the relationship would mean the annulment of individual autonomy and separation. The container should however guarantee acceptance and welcoming of each partner's potential, drawing on their preceding experience of being contained by the primary object.

Often couples look for help because the relationship they are currently building has become not a container but more like a suffocating prison. Meltzer (1992) defines as a 'claustrum' a relationship that is characterised by reciprocal projections deriving from an omnipotent phantasy of intrusion into another person. It is thus desirable for the relationship to be flexible enough to enable the necessary transformations of the couple and of the individuals that comprise it, and to be stable enough to protect it from the anxieties of change, and to have boundaries, privacy and exclusivity.

Mary Morgan (2005) defines as a 'creative couple' a situation in which the psychic development of each member finds itself at a stage leading to the development of something new, even external to themselves. The relationship becomes experienced subjectively as a source of support and a resource, something that can be transformed, resulting in a third thing that is bigger than the sum of its parts.: 'The partners feel that they have something that links them, something they can go back to and that contains them as individuals, something that they are able to take care of, and at the same time they can imagine it taking care of them' (Morgan, 2005, p. 48).

If, in couple therapy, the relationship itself is the patient, the separate identity of each partner will establish itself, while at the same time a third presence will be sensed that is not dominated by that of either. Pickering (2011), referring to Ogden's concept of 'analytical third', writes of this intersubjective third that:

> In a couple relationship, there is a way in which the coming together of two individuals gives rise to a third form of subjectivity, which emerges through their coupling. A couple contains the two individuals, each with their separate

personality, but there is a sense of a third presence circling around the two partners, revealed (or concealed) by the communications of the individuals, but controlled by neither. (Pickering, 2011, p. 55)

This new aspect is located in the dialectical tension between individual subjectivities and is not a static entity; it is an evolving experience, both conscious and unconscious, in a state of continuous change. It is perceived differently by each partner, though each (partially) entrusts their own separate individuality to it.

Bion's dynamic theory of thinking offers a very fertile model here (Bianchini & Dallanegra, 2010, 2011). The containment of the relationship allows the reconfiguration of raw unprocessed proto-emotions, in unconscious phantasies, myths, reconstructions, changes of perspective, receiving the thought that is outside the thinker. In order for this to happen it is necessary that each partner be prepared to tolerate the vacuum of un-thinkableness so that beta-elements can be decompressed through receptive-dreaming abilities – the reverie of the other. The function of the container is to share the emotional experience with the other loved person; the act of caring makes the emotions more tolerable. This process develops in both directions: container and contained work reciprocally, in a state of mutual tension. In the couple, its functions are symmetrical, reversible, and in continuous reciprocal co-construction. When there is reciprocation, a couple can function creatively in a continuing expansion of new containers and contents. The roles of container and contained alternate between the pair, so each gains enrichment by new qualities and truths, nourishing their own development through this constant dialogue. It can only be done by the acceptance of aspects of one's self and the other which may be deeply disturbing (Gabbard & Ogden, 2009).

When contact and proximity arouse excessive quantities of proto-emotional states in the partners, an unbalance may be created between the development of the container and the growth of its contents. In the following example we may see a possible case of this happening.

Claudio and Daniela argue all the time and they are always on the brink of splitting up. Their one-year-old daughter cries incessantly and does not let them sleep. It seems impossible to find a container for their anger and for the inconsolable crying of Rosita. There is never a moment of calm. Claudio attacks Daniela aggressively, even in front of the therapist, by insulting her in demeaning and mortifying ways; Daniela weeps, releasing all her desperation. In this way Claudio uses the space to vent his anger while the therapist tries to contain him and make contact with Daniela again.

Claudio belongs to a wealthy family where the environment was always troubled by rivalry with his brother who was eighteen years older than him, a dictatorial father, and a weak mother who sought refuge in her headaches. Daniela left her family at fourteen in order to study in another city and could never rely on any emotional or financial support. She managed to achieve a good professional level of which she is proud.

The couple came to us because they were not able to manage their child's crying and in order to understand how this increases the emotional conflict between them. It emerged how in the history of both they lacked the experience of excessive and intolerable emotions being contained. Within the couple, Claudio always tries to take command, and Daniela can only withdraw desperate and wounded, leaving him lonely, which makes Claudio's anger even more violent and Daniela's withdrawal even deeper.

The request for help to learn how to deal with Rosita's crying corresponds to an unconscious and parallel request to understand and console the personal suffering that they are only able to express through his shouting and her silence. We are presented with two 'contents' that both need containing. The configuration emerges of a psychic functioning characterised by hyper-contents that try to find acceptance in a hypo-container: a situation that harms the relationship and each partner because neither of them is receptive to the other.

We believe therefore that the couple therapist's role is to facilitate the expansion of the relation container<–>contained in order to augment its capacity and equilibrium, so that the exchange between the partners can become more thinkable, and emotions able to find a place in a reciprocal (even if precarious) dynamic of mutual dependence.

Conclusion

It becomes apparent how the map of personal development drawn up by an individual is liable to be sprinkled with blind spots, which resurface during the failure of any of the projects of adulthood. In the case of the couple relationship, each partner needs to work on both their internal dynamics and on the dynamic created by the partnership: the interweaving of the 'sense of self' and the 'sense of us' (Norsa & Zavattini, 1997). However this interweaving does not imply confusion or blurring.

The model we use in therapy is based on the idea that the meeting of two people creates a different 'third reality', and the goal is to inspire the emergence of a 'marital self' (Eiguer, 2008), in which the partners, alongside the therapist, learn to observe their own specific attributes and how these can contribute to a reciprocal, active interchange. New ways of thinking, enabled by the therapist, enable a reconstruction or reformulation of the self, the internal objects, and the relationship with the other. Although in certain cases individual therapy might be recommended, a joint encounter favours a wider vision, taking into account interactive dynamics, and gives unknown parts of the self an opportunity to find a voice which might otherwise go undetected.

We can therefore imagine the therapy as a transformative fly-wheel, concentrating on balance and fluctuation, in which the relation becomes generative if it is successful in providing the patients with certain tools that are lacking. Through our observational capacity we try to note and make contact with unrecognised emotions and contain them through a new lens (Gabbard, 2003), based on a shared moment of thought in which even painful emotion becomes tolerable to all, by means of this constructive exchange.

To a certain extent the analyst's mind must experience the same illness as the patient, as it is the keystone of the analytic field that comprises all the dynamic elements. His or her own inner world must be actively engaged. The couple's distress affects us and we cannot avoid it; it is only eased by helping patients acquire the tools to transform it for themselves (Civitarese, 2008; Ferro & Vender, 2010). The equipment of the analyst needs to include, according to Grotstein, 'a function of *passion*, the analyst's submersion into his own subjectivity to locate matching experiences and emotions that resonate with the analysand's emotional experience and convey credible patterns and configurations' (2007, p. 91)

For the joint couple session is shaped by the receptivity of the therapist-as-object. The 'circularity principle' (as seen in the primary relationship when there is an appropriate response from the maternal object) creates a space in which the self, the other, the couple, and the therapist can be thought about and spoken of together. A group comes into existence in the room which takes note of many different points of view, that can enter into dialogue rather than excluding one other. The therapist has to take care particularly that no impasse occurs, as happens when participants cease to listen to each other and resort to blaming the other. A special type of commitment and availability is required, as with all these sources of conflict, doubts and questions are multiplied and it is difficult to create a developmental space.

As will be discussed in the next chapter, the therapist needs to take an equilateral approach, meaning that engagement is necessary but from an appropriate and impartial distance. This is necessary because the intensity of the emotional flux and the complexity of the dynamics that arise during the session entail a strong risk of creating confusion and becoming involved in collusion with one partner or the other.

CHAPTER THREE

Equilaterality: the structure of the couple and the mental state of the therapist

Maria Adelaide Lupinacci and Giulio Cesare Zavattini

> Each personality is a world in himself, a company of many.
> (Joan Riviere, 1952, p. 317)

Observing the couple relationship in the privileged context of psychoanalytical psychotherapy, one is from the beginning struck by the substantiality and extent of the spatial element. The concept of relationship itself implies the extension of psychic space, since we don't deal only with the internal space of the individual but also with the imaginary non-sensuous place where the relationship unfolds and the internal worlds with their objects and emotions meet and interlink.

We think the best metaphor proposed so far for describing the spatial structure of the couple, allowing us to follow its fluctuations and dynamics, is the triangle. Naturally the idea of triangularity and of the third person immediately brings to mind the oedipal conflict, and we will try to use this in our explanation of the metaphor.

After Melanie Klein (1928) pointed out how one of the fundamental components of the oedipal conflict in the child

41

was the sense of exclusion from the parents (in addition to the desire for possession of the mother, and rivalry with the father, as noted by Freud), other authors have taken up this topic and have emphasised the sense of exclusion (Britton 1989, 2000; Emde, 1991). The complex of emotions that awaken in the child when he begins to realise that the two most important people in his life are engaged in an intimacy that excludes him, stimulates his curiosity. This acts as a catalyst in his psychic development because it enables him to view himself in relation to others outside himself.

We find Britton's (1989) elaboration of the oedipal conflict as a 'triangular space' to be particularly useful. Britton describes how the child faced by a difficult oedipal complex has a double developmental challenge: to tolerate the pain of recognising the intimate sexual bond between the parents, from which he is excluded, and at the same time to preserve the different quality of his own love for each individual parent, in this way process- ing the loss of his omnipotent phantasy of total possession. This double process has many consequences that can help emotional growth and extend mental and imaginary space. If the child can accept the privacy of his parents' relationship he can begin to understand different types of relationships, some of which he might always be excluded from, but in others he will be included; and others again he will be able to initiate himself. A special type of object relation is formed in which one is not a protagonist, and a 'third position' is gained 'from which object relationships can be observed. This provides us with a capacity for seeing ourselves in interaction with others and for entertain- ing another point of view whilst retaining our own, for reflect- ing on ourselves whilst being ourselves' (Britton, 1989, p. 86).

The triangular space thus opens the way to a more complex dimensionality of the mind that is co-extensive with an expanded container–contained model (Bion, 1963): the contained, bene- fiting from containment, is able to take on new contents. The child, though pained by the realisation that he is excluded, can envisage a mother separate from himself, and the separateness of the parental relationship on which he depends physically and emotionally. This extended model implies that in an adult relationship, especially a couple relationship, a person does not only benefit himself from containment, but can also become a better container. Britton linked the failure to internalise the oedipal triangle to a prior failure to make a significant dyadic bond with the mother, even if separation is tolerated. In the worst cases this results from a failure of maternal containment, with the father perceived as a persecutor that keeps attacking the dyadic relationship. In more benign situations, defensive illusions deny the creativity of the parental couple and obscure psychic reality. With couples, it is therefore important to understand what internal structures have already been established and what relationships have been internalised when the child moves on from the primal relationship and later the oedipal situation. The person's later relationships are founded on the paradigm of these unconscious internal object relations.

For example, it might happen that a woman scarred by a painful childhood experience of abandonment may unconsciously search for a partner who can offer a stable and faithful refuge, but all her life tries to find in him a secret tendency to betray or disappoint, so that she can reaffirm her masochistic fears, with the secondary triumph of being able to unmask him. Equally, a man who is daily accused of this might have the unconscious phantasy that his wife is a castrating and suffocating mother, reaffirming his own deep fears and re-enacting a disappointing internal relationship.

In terms of adult relationships, the partners in a couple depend emotionally not only on the reciprocal containment they each offer the other (Lupinacci 1994; Lupinacci & Zavattini 2002, 2004), but also on the state of the relationship created between them. We think all this needs to be seen in a more complex way than Freud's classical delineation of partners being chosen according to similarity or contrast, and is more complex even than Klein's view of projective identification. Both these views imply a too linear reading, with the other as a space into which aspects of the self are put for containment. The picture in which each partner uses the other to project idealised or persecutory aspects represents an important aspect of psychic reality, however it lacks the idea of the availability of a mutual object held between them (Puget, 2010; Zavattini & Gigli, 2010; Gigli, Velotti & Zavattini, 2012a, 2012b). It is necessary to understand the intertwining and mutuality in terms of a shared psychic reality, as was very well described by Dicks in his seminal study (1967).

The basis of the analyst–patient relationship with couples therefore posits the existence of a third entity that is created by both partners, but that doesn't exhaust their potentialities. As Ruszczynski suggests (1996, 2005) we can think of the marital triangle itself as something created by both partners with their relationship as the third element, a symbolic product of their coupling, with its own identity. This idea is already present in Bion's (1970) container–contained model, with its potential for creating either a constructive or a destructive third entity. We will return to this later in the negative relationship (–R).

So it is necessary to see the marital relationship (or any other intimate long-lasting relationship) not as a simple addition of the internal worlds of each partner but as a new production born from an unconscious interlocking. The logic of the intervention with couples requires us to go beyond the interpretation directed at the individual, following the idea that the dynamics need to be read in terms of a bipersonal field (Baringer & Baringer, 1969; Ferro, 2002b) shared between the partners, that influences the here-and-now of the session (Zavattini & Lupinacci, 2004). The setting creates a scenario in which a pattern of meaning can emerge from this virtual space, with the characteristics of that particular field (Zavattini, 2006).

The specialist literature on couple therapy on an object–relations basis holds that the transference between the members of a couple is the central complex feature to be examined, and is characterised by a fluctuating tendency that makes it particularly difficult to comprehend (Scharff & Scharff, 1991; Ruszczynski & Fisher, 1995, Norsa & Zavattini, 1997; Fisher, 1999; Clulow, 2001, 2009; Velotti & Zavattini, 2008; Scharff, 2011; Gigli, Velotti & Zavattini, 2012a). The psychoanalysis of couples has shown that the interlocking of internal worlds can be considered a type of natural transference relationship. As Gosling (1968) puts it, 'falling in love is one of the most surprising examples of transference'.

It has been suggested that we can usefully see work with couples as taking place on two levels: the transference between the couple, and their transference to the therapist, both as a couple and as individuals. The presence of both levels makes particular the work with couples compared to that with individual patients. In particular it can make it harder for the psychoanalyst to maintain a position of separateness and equilibrium (Morgan, 2001) when interpreting the internal state of the patient. The risk is of emotional collusion with one or the other partner thereby falling into confusion over their motivation, and owing to conscious or unconscious bias, slip into errors of judgement.

The marital triangle: equilateral and scalene

We would like to consider the couple relationship as one which is symmetric rather than asymmetric as between child and mother (or caregiver). There are two equals who each expect to benefit from mutual containment and enrichment, thus forming a conjugal 'triangle' together with their relationship which can be seen as a discreet entity (Ruszczynski, 1993) – an identity that might interfere with the individual desires or needs of any individual partner. To become aware of this third entity or vertex can be disturbing, as it brings to view both separateness from the other, and dependency on the relationship. There may be anxiety that the triangular space may destroy phantasies of ideal union or twinship.

Or there may be a suspicion that the triangular space is unbalanced: that one of the partners dominates the space. When a narcissistic relationship blocks the image of the other, what is unrecognised or denied is also the sense of the value of the relationship itself as the third element in the conjugal triangle. Lacking a third position, individual and couple growth is difficult to achieve (Morgan, 2001). Or the conjugal triangle may itself become pathological or dysfunctional in itself: negated, or idealized, or unbalanced, to the detriment of one of the members – for example, the downtrodden wife of a husband who is violent, or always absent at the pub, or a workaholic. Or the intimacy of the conjugal relationship can be dependent on a child who is given the role of keeping the couple together; in this case the triangle is flattened – the child disappears as a person in himself and becomes an adjunct to the couple, who are adhesively joined. The aim is to preserve habits and continuity without engaging in any productive exchange.

The quality of triangularity can also oscillate within the life cycle of the marital couple, or of any intimate emotional relationship. For example as Freud (1921) revealed, the classic theme of the honeymoon period is nearly psychotic in terms of its mutual idealisation and will later need to be modified by a vision that is more realistic and based on the work done by the interlinking of the partners. When one person is dominant there is a linear relationship; when two are equal, the situation is more complex, hence its representation by a triangle. The triangle covers the changing couple dynamics very well since when any of the vertices changes so does the value of the figure as a whole. We therefore have equilateral or scalene (unequal-sided) triangles, depending on the position of the vertices A and B (the partners) in relation to the vertex of reference (R, the relationship).

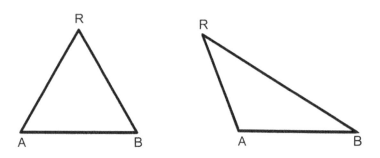

This means that there may be a balance; or that one or other of the couple may dominate or absorb the relationship (R) to the detriment of the other partner, maybe partially or temporarily, or in relation to an individual problem. For example, in the relatively benign case of a well-matched middle-aged couple, Mr and Mrs T, a serious illness of his mother (a dominating woman) invaded the space of their relationship, moving the vertex of their interests towards placating the husband's damaged and greedy maternal object. This event disturbed the distance the husband had maintained towards his persecutory object, inducing him to marginalise the needs of his wife and the relationship. So the triangle had become scalene, risking a crisis in the couple. In this case the pathology of the conjugal triangle could be explained quite easily, and the tension be resolved in a fairly short time. In other cases the unbalance may be more rigid; the other can unconsciously collude in the face of internal or external events, creating a condition of stable but chronic suffering. This is the case of Emma and Giorgio whom we will discuss later.

As observed by many authors (Ruszczynski & Fisher, 1995; Fisher, 1999; Ruszczynski, 2005; Zavattini, 2006) another possible third is the couple's analyst: and someone who can observe the relationship from another vertex whilst at the same time being part of it in so far as the couple transference (the product of the relationship) is gathered to him. When the couple become aware of the importance of the analyst's role in maintaining the equilaterality of the triangle, they also become aware of their dependence on the therapist and the therapeutic situation for the quality of their relationship and also up to a point for the pursuit of their individual destinies within the relationship itself. This dependency can be feared and arouse hostile emotions towards the therapist. Another fear is that the analyst may not be able to ensure equal weight and recognition to both partners, but may bias his vertex towards one or the other. This is one of the most common fears of patients engaging in couple therapy, felt at the commencement and also as it continues.

Changing triangularity in a couple

We would like to give an example of the nature of triangularity in a couple, Emma and Giorgio. The relationship had initially found a symbolic container in the place of their first meeting where they fell in love, the city in the north where they both worked. Often couples have a very clear vision of the place where they first noticed the other. This memory and/or phantasy involves expectations not only of the other person but of 'us', the two together.

Emma and Giorgio were united by lively intelligence and interests, an unconventional vision of the world, and the desire to get away from their own families whom they both regarded as difficult. They were both aged 30 and so far had not found their own sense of identity outside their families. They realised they shared similar anxieties and defences. So from their first meeting they were both convinced there should be an emotional bond between them. Giorgio had always avoided committing to a longterm relationship, then rejection by a woman made him both more needy and less defensive. Giorgio's courtship attracted Emma, who was very insecure in her relationships with the opposite sex, and needy for affection. So Emma's hunger for affection and Giorgio's need (mixed with fear and hostility) for a serious relationship came together to create the unconscious psychic space of their relationship. But there was more to it than that.

Emma's availability, which attracted the disappointed and frustrated Giorgio, was linked to an unconscious tendency to identify herself with an indulgent mother (very different from her own mother whom she found mean, tyrannical and violent). Giorgio was very practical and appreciated Emma's direct and unconventional manners and intellectual qualities. Emma hoped that he would be an ideal figure (not necessarily masculine, in fact at the end of the day quite asexual), who would support her in shaking off this terrible mother; she also blamed her father for not defending her and leaving her to her mother's caprices.

Emma's vitality and outspokenness, coming from a rough family background, reassured Giorgio since she seemed so different from the conventional mother to whom he had had a very strong bond in his early childhood, but from whom he separated quite dramatically later. In fact Giorgio accused his mother of being a bourgeois conformist who was crushed by the demands of his bullying and unfaithful father. However on the unconscious level, what emerged during the therapy was a deeper, ancient resentment that his mother had not really been affectionate or really understood him as a child: that she had replaced him with his brothers. Emma was sufficiently different from this maternal image; she was not bound by conventional limitations. Unconsciously Giorgio asked Emma not to impose any boundaries on him, not even those of a tender mother or father as required by the oedipal situation. Exuberant and eager Emma, who also disliked boundaries and had her own problems with them, seemed the perfect match.

In this partly conscious, partly unconscious intertwining of expectations, relational models, shared issues and defence mechanisms, the hostile relationship of both of them with their mother and their own 'difficult' families – the fractured parental couple for Emma and the denied (negated) parents for Giorgio – neither of them could internally locate a sufficiently good and stable internal triangle.

For Emma and Giorgio the triangle of their initial relationship seemed to maintain an equilateral position in the sense that the relationship between them seemed to contain the rationale, the need, and potential power to rebalance old object relation problems. Nevertheless their union, despite some solid and realistic libidinous features, was mainly based on the expectation of using the other to escape (and eventually conquer) their own infantile persecutory object. They felt themselves to be in an idealised twinship that unified them against a common enemy but that (as shown later on) couldn't tolerate an object other than the self or genuinely separate. The phantasy of twinship is different from an equilibrium which is sufficiently solid for an equilateral triangle to exist. The unresolved internal relationship with the primal objects, above all the failed maternal containment, especially in Emma, contributed to making the narcissistic aspects of the partners (Fisher 1999) very strong. 'This is what I'm like!' had become Emma's assertion on many occasions. 'You can't tell me what to do!' Giorgio would thunder threateningly when he heard his wife demanding more respect for their relationship, protesting against his unfaithfulness which had become habitual.

This narcissistic structure of internal relations made awareness of the third dimension tenuous. The precarious equilibrium of the conjugal triangle was disturbed by the impact of the 'facts of life' (Money-Kyrle, 1961): living together, birth of children, awareness of time passing, and by the demands of the inner world. At this point, given the great complexity to be found in every interlocking couple, we will mention some features of the conjugal triangle that will help us understand better the increasingly scalene configuration of Giorgio and Emma's relationship.

From the time the children were born, Emma's infantile voracious emotionality, intolerant of separation, led her into a partial female identity, founded on being a completely available mother, geared totally to bringing up the children, on whom she projected all her own needy infantile but also bullying parts, whilst becoming less sensitive to the requirements of the husband and their relationship.

Giorgio remained partially excluded from this reconfiguration of the couple after the arrival of the children. He had never coped very well with having a close relationship and now he started a series of affairs, identifying with a partial masculinity, phallic and narcissistic, in the meantime building up a violent bitterness toward Emma in whom he felt extremely disappointed. In his view she turned from being a quickwitted nonconformist adolescent partner to being a suffocating mother or needy dependent child. As an alternative to this Giorgio imposed an alternative structure on the couple, locating his phallic sexuality outside the marriage. Through his unfaithfulness he attacked not only his wife but through her his idea of his own mother; and also set up a rivalry with the bullying father whom he feared, whilst at the same time trying to distance himself from a relationship in which he felt himself the weaker partner.

In this way they both installed a scalene relationship, each claiming the balance of power for themselves. By the time they contacted the psychoanalyst – a woman – the situation between them had totally collapsed; he had lovers; they continuously argued bitterly about everything; however they still didn't consider separating. 'The discussions between us always arrive at a dead end. We need a third.' Intuitively Emma and Giorgio were handing over their relationship to a third – the analyst.

Variations on triangularity in therapy

We would like now to consider further the 'R' (relationship) vertex, with R represented by the therapist. In particular we would like to examine how R may become distorted during psychoanalytic psychotherapy, owing to the pressures on the countertransference of a narcissistic coupling between the A and B vertices (the partners). This can create a situation we might call −R, using the minus sign in the same way that Bion does, borrowing it from algebra, in which 'a change of sign, say for a line AB, represents a change in sense of the line' (Bion, 1962, p. 52). The meaning of an emotional link becomes inverted, that is, negated. Bion considered the fundamental developmental emotional links to be love, hate, and knowledge (LHK), and the defences against this emotionality to be seen as negative links (−LHK). Analogously, we propose that within the conjugal triangle there can exist a −R vertex, when the triangle is equilateral, but the joint interaction of the partners is one of silent mutual agreement to attack and negate the relationship. The anti-libidinous orientation in which they jointly move is upheld by a confirmed misunderstanding. In couple therapy this condition manifests itself in a joint attack on the therapist's function and capacity to think, and on the therapeutic setting.

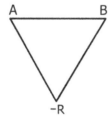

To clarify this configuration we will return to Emma and Giorgio. One time the psychoanalyst arrived five minutes late and commented on the unease they felt at her delay. The two partners minimised what happened but in the form of an ironic attack, devaluing the analyst's function. They said they didn't mind, but in a way that made the importance of the punctuality of the therapist seem ridiculous. Emma, who gives piano lessons, says that even with the children she is very flexible about time; and she looks at the analyst as if she were very narrow-minded. Giorgio becomes very ironic and says it's not a problem for him: 'But maybe it is for you, doctor.' They both laugh.

The problem of time, owing to their own habitual lateness, was a longstanding bone of contention. The therapist is annoyed but also a little dazed. For a moment she feels she is not quite sure what her ideas are; she feels a sense of humiliation like a child exposed to the mocking laughter of insensitive adults. However she manages to comment on the fact they really can't bear to be precise about time, and maybe they feel about their own relationship in the same way, like a constriction. Both of them deny this, and Giorgio is particularly entrenched in his position. There is a deep silence. After a while, nonchalantly, they both say they were thinking about their own preoccupations. So they had returned to their own little narcissistic worlds; their dependence on each other and on the therapeutical relationship for the solving of their problems is denied and dropped.

The simplest and most common situation in which a triangle stays balanced but negative is when the couple collude to exclude the psychoanalyst from the situation, often catching him or her in a tricky dialogue or argument which prevents him from thinking about what is going on between the three of them.

What we wish to illustrate is how the narcissism of the two partners can collude to keep their relationship out of the picture, or to move it away from intimacy and thought in a direction of −R. And as here, the therapist and the analytic relationship are also excluded by this narcissistic alliance. This movement towards misunderstanding is quite different from an adult mutual decision between the couple to split up. The therapist's function is to ensure the relationship can be thought about and kept in equilibrium; and sometimes a successful therapy can take the form of helping the partners to dissolve an unsustainable and imprisoning bond from which they need to free themselves. In the case of an unbalanced 'scalene' couple such a decision could paradoxically be considered both the first and the last co-operative, positive one of their relationship.

To continue with the account of the '−R' session with Emma and Giorgio. After the silence, Giorgio teases his wife about her intention to visit some friends in the north. It is the first time she has been away from the family on her own and in a sense it is an achievement. Emma replies by complaining about Romans and the 'messy' life in the city where they live (he is from Rome, she is from the north), says she is very tired of taking care of everyone – they all depend on her and she is not that strong. Giorgio replies 'Well stay there then – and stop complaining.' There is a harsh contrast between her sad, depressed look and his ironic, triumphant one. The painful matters of separation, exclusion, and neediness, are evident.

These matters were earlier projected into the therapist and could not be processed because of their mutual collusion; still linger and are tossed between the partners. However Emma's complaint that everyone depends on her tells us something more. The therapist knows that probably it is a reference to the last few sessions, when they had touched a deeply hidden area in their relationship, in which Giorgio's secret phantasies emerged in a dream of a harem courtyard, of unrestricted phallic excitement and wild sexuality, a phantasy that was also a defence against his anxieties in his relations with women. The theme of a secret space, introduced by Giorgio, brought to light Emma's own hidden phantasy space, as manager of the 'children's room'. This clarified her identification with a warm, welcoming, idealised mother, who indulged everyone's demands and desires. Into her children Emma projected her own angry, depressed and greedy child self, cooking and eating huge quantities of food. Giorgio also found refuge in this secret part of Emma for his own depressed and frozen child self, as an alternative to the phallic father to whom he had turned in adolescence, and who had been unfaithful to his mother. In this identification, Giorgio had seen him as an accomplice in his own adolescent exploits, and at the same time a man-to-man supporter of his work and studies.

Part of Emma's unconscious phantasy was reparative, another part represented an omnipotent belief in being stronger than the women of the harem and than Giorgio's bad mother, believing therefore she would be able to rescue him. For both of them the secret imaginary space (the harem, the children's room) got in the way of intimacy in their relationship. Emma had become more mother than wife, neglecting herself physically; her ambitions were all directed towards motherhood not

to marital relations. Outside this ambit, Giorgio searched for
sexual adventures, finding partners who were often weak or
subjugated.

The analyst, bearing in mind this recent material, then
observes that maybe the city in which Emma is no longer happy
is also a mental space in which she doesn't feel comfortable: it
refers to her emotional state and relationships. The phantasy is
of rescuing her husband from the harem, since she is the one
who takes care of everyone. Giorgio, pointing out everything he
does for his wife, quickly attacks the analyst and she immediately
realises that her intervention was unbalanced and incomplete.
She had let herself be seduced into Emma's orbit, identifying
with her omnipotent phantasy of rescuer, imagining that she
could herself rescue Emma from her secret 'room' where she
exhausts herself in taking care of everyone. In this way, we lost
sight of the actual relationship, in which the couple colluded in
a mutual exploitation.

Giorgio exploits Emma through seeking excitement in his
adventures with groups of 'boys' who humiliate women; yet
at the same time wanting the maternal warmth of a home and
family, to which he always returns. Emma exploits Giorgio by
projecting her 'mean' mother into him, yet she derives security and material benefits from him, and children whom he
didn't want. She uses him to feel superior to her own mother
and the analyst, neglecting the relationship and Giorgio's wish
that she take care of her femininity and physical appearance.
Giorgio's sexual vagaries thus also function as part of Emma's
identifications: specifically, her narcissistic identification with
the super-indulgent ideal mother who forgives all trespasses.
All this had not been perceived or understood by the therapist
at this point, and the triangle had become scalene owing to her
interpretative imbalance which leaned more towards one of the
couple, Emma.

Going back to the material, we could have interpreted that
Emma was trying to distance herself from the shared or reciprocal disorder in the relationship – the 'messy city' in which they
both live – and from the disorder of an attack on the 'here and
now' of the psychoanalytic session in which the whole sequence

started. How to explain this momentary loss of equilibrium in the therapist? In part, Emma with her overtired, dishevelled appearance aroused a maternal instinct in the therapist, and it could have been useful to have investigated further the topic of the 'children's room' at that point, not just the 'harem court-yard'. In addition, the analyst had been disturbed by the initial joint attack on the therapeutic setting after she arrived late. The couple's hypocritical reaction to this revealed that they were attacking the relationship by means of an attack on the analyst's capacity for thought, an example of –K. The analyst needs to be in a position of observing rather than participating in the rela-tionship, and she temporarily lost her equidistant objectivity and pushed the triangle into a scalene shape. By momentarily losing this position the thinking function was dislodged and the analyst was attracted to the defensive configuration put in place by the couple to conserve their mutual dependency, hence resulting in an unbalanced interpretation.

Both members of the couple had an unbalanced internal triangulation in their masculine and feminine qualities, in their picture of the parental couple. We have seen how Giorgio had gradually distanced himself from his wife as a woman in the same way that he internally distanced himself from his mother, despising her whilst idealising the father as a comrade, an inter-nal accomplice. For Emma, the mother was internally split into persecutory and idealised, while the father was a weak and absent figure in the family picture, disconnected from the mother, so that Emma's own femininity was completely absorbed in and limited to the idea of an overabundant, unbounded mater-nity. In Emma's mind the role of the male had become one of compensating for what her mother had not given her.

Emma and Giorgio thus colluded in leaving the other to live in a world made of either phallic males or over-maternal women, rather than being an authentically creative couple. Their respec-tive narcissism prompted an evacuation of anxiety, triumphing over persecutory internal objects, especially the mother, rather than uniting in a positive way. A scalene configuration was then intensely projected into the psychoanalytic situation and momentarily not contained in the transference by the analyst.

We also need to remember that the mocked and excluded child was also projected into the analyst as if by destructive parents, re-enacting the 'parasitic' or lying relationship spoken of by Bion (1970). They enacted a phantasy like the myth of Oedipus' killer parents, who do not wish to be disturbed by infantile dependency (Lupinacci, 1994). All this contributed to the analyst's projective counter-identification with Emma's 'children's room' and a solely 'feminine' view of the couple relationship.

Conclusions

As we have seen, analytic work with couples is distinctive in that it deals with two people involved in an equal relationship. For the therapist it is therefore important to pay attention to the balance of interventions, whether in the form of interpretations, questions or comments. We call this a triangular space in which every member can reflect on their own needs in relation to the other, and on the requirements of the relationship. The aim is to make the space positive and equilateral rather than scalene or negatively equilateral (−R).

The triangularity also refers to the quality of the unconscious interlock between two internal worlds, and the mirror of its dynamics. There may always be psychic forces within one or the other partner, or both, that will try to destroy any resolution and damage the relationship. This entails the possibility of the analyst being drawn in and overwhelmed by the unconscious forces. Taking care of the triangular space means dealing with moments of crisis or unbalance, and lack of emotional synchronicity, that need further reflection and a capacity to tolerate ambivalence. Whatever the outcome it will provide an important source of information at countertransference level.

There is a fear that even in the therapeutic session the triangle can become scalene. This needs to be at the forefront of observing the interactions of the transference and one's own countertransference, and in the way interpretations are presented (Zavattini, 2001a, 2001b; Santona & Zavattini, 2005). Although the masculine and feminine in psychological makeup are strong organisers of a capacity to tolerate difference and otherness, a long training and deep reflection are necessary to cope with the anxieties that are stirred up in the sessions, and that may result in partiality. The repercussions on technique of the strong emotions aroused by the two triangular shapes in couple therapy represent one of the main challenges to the therapist. We need to consider with great care the timing and delivery of interventions in the session, discarding the logic of blame and evoking rather the phantasies and anxieties regarding the link between the couple: for example, the anxiety that each partner has of being eaten up, used or obliterated not only by the other but by the relationship itself. The technique of interpretation should be able to include both shared and individual dynamics, and put the couple in a position to experience aspects of their own subjectivity which they have split off into the relationship.

We believe that equilaterality goes beyond the important concept of neutrality, to also involve taking care of the third element called into being by the partners. Couples in therapy recognise the special nature of the experience they encounter, very different from the claustrophobic, irrational atmosphere that is generally created by couples in crisis. They believe they have found a place and time where they can at least present what they think and feel, guaranteed by the functioning of the analyst. In this space, talking – which often has an evacuative, projective and manipulative quality – regains the quality of communication, about the self and above all the relationship. An equilateral as distinct from linear functioning is one in which each partner contributes an aspect of their internal object and their associated phantasies about the internal couple. It is enabled by the presence of the third party, the analyst, who through the setting offers containment for these complex dynamics.

But as we have seen the analyst can unconsciously take on an unbalanced position within his own countertransference and act out within the setting, and this in fact frequently happens. So it is important to have a suitable theoretical model to comprehend it clinically and deal with it technically, which means the analyst needs to continuously examine his personal oedipal conflict, and be conscious of the anxieties aroused by the pressure made on the countertransference. This is an task that continues lifelong (Lupinacci & Zabbatini, 2004). Doing this, he can ensure not just neutrality but the equanimity that ensures adequate recognition of the couple itself as the patient. He must continually try to seek out and maintain the 'third position' (Britton, 1989) from which to observe the interactions. This fundamental element allows the unfolding of the transference and provides the conditions suitable for interpretation. Mary Morgan (2001) describes this orientation of the analyst as having a 'couple state of mind'. This refers to a capacity to keep in mind the relationship as an entity in itself, not just keeping in mind both partners. It can then inspire a similar state of mind in the couple themselves, so that for each of them there will be a chance of perceiving simultaneously themselves, the needs of the other, and the relationship between them. This can alleviate the reciprocal projective identification that would have brought an element of paralysis to the relationship and that would also interfere with the psychic state of any children there may be.

The couple relationship thus organises two internal worlds by means of an inter- and intra-subjective dimension, forming not only a couple but also the basis for a complete restructuring of the personality. However this does not mean (especially in psychopathology) that there could not also be a rigid, adherent aspect carried over from the previous experience, hard to transform, that we attempt to resolve by delegating the problem to the relationship. In such a case the couple relationship is given responsibility for resolving the self's incoherence (an illusion). Thus we need to understand what structures have been set up in the relationship, which is being used by both to fight old wars but with a new enemy, their partner. Without either being aware, they can end up in a new intersubjective collusion, a *folie à deux* generated by the encounter of their two internal organisations. The therapeutic objective requires each partner to recognise their projections, to find out how these aspects of themselves are experienced, and how they may be tolerated (Fisher, 1999), so that we can encourage the development in each of a more coherent, integrated and autonomous self.

The triangular model has many useful possibilities for expansion. Many variations can occur in the triple setting (the couple with one therapist), and further possibilities arise with a quadruple setting (with two therapists) as shall be discussed in the next chapter.

CHAPTER FOUR

The therapist at work: technical matters

Marina Capello

Human beings build too many walls and not enough bridges.
(Isaac Newton)

In the previous chapters we highlighted the theoretical elements that are specific to couple therapy. The change in point of view, compared to individual psychoanalysis, influences the technique which needs to change in line with it. In this chapter we will explore this extension. Whilst in individual therapy only one person can talk about the absent partner, as an internal object, in the couple setting the therapist has to concern himself with both actual partners, and to distinguish the real object from the represented (internalised) object. It is not easy to see the boundary between the two realities, as one may be faced with a very strong projective identification, in which an aspect of the self – either idealised or negated – is handed over very forcefully to the other, who finds himself becoming like the picture that the partner has of him. The realistic aspect of the partner is confused by the projections that enter into him or her.

This significant change of viewpoint is the real subject foundation of couple therapy technique, implying a different vision of the setting and of transference–countertransference dynamics. The work with couples or families has traditionally been the territory of systems theory, especially with regard to real modes of behaviour and interaction. The systems school starts from the premise that the family is the object of observation, and the interactions the object of intervention (M. Selvini Palazzoli et al., 1975); therefore it uses a type of setting whose theoretical model is based on real interactions and hence seeks objectivity as far as is possible. He who uses a psychoanalytical model on the other hand, works from a viewpoint that values subjectivity, using countertransference as a work tool. When a therapist works in a couple setting a series of wide and complex intersubjective phenomena are aroused – feelings, phantasies, and thoughts – on which he is required to reflect. He therefore needs to maintain a model in which the focus is on intersubjectivity rather than on behaviour, but which still observes real interactions between the people who are present. Listening to accounts of dreams and descriptions of events, he needs to build a series of hypotheses about the internal worlds of each partner, and constantly shift attention between his observations and his hypotheses about their internal organisations.

In psychoanalytic theory the setting is considered the first and most important factor. It is the framework in which psychoanalytic practice is enabled to unfold and develop in a logical way. To briefly recapitulate its history: the reconstructive model, based on the analysis of the past experience of the patient, privileged a setting that allowed regression and the emergence of transference. The concept of the analyst as mirror (Freud, 1912) arose as a result of Freud's need to give scientific legitimacy to the theory he was building, and his worry that the analyst could be influenced by his own subjectivity. However this orientation often ended up encouraging a cold and detached attitude in the analyst. With the development of object relations theory, psychoanalysis shifted from a reconstructive to a constructive view which is aware of the 'here and now' and of intersubjective relationships. The task of the analyst therefore is not only to maintain the setting, but also to facilitate its emergence. We can distinguish between the external setting (rules about place, time and transactions between patient and therapist) and the internal setting, given by the mental attitude of the analyst, which constitutes the basic logic of the relationship.

While the external setting describes the conditions which are suitable for events to unfold between analyst and patient, and which allow the emergence of phantasies, identifications, defences and emotions, the analyst is the dynamic containing structure that enables the transformation. So the task of the therapist is to refine and maintain the mental state that allows him to listen to the patient and himself and to confront the pain. It should be noted that this view does not give the framework secondary importance; indeed some authors believe that it makes it more rigorous and at the same time more problematic because it is not just given, it is continuously recreated. Thus Grinberg (1981) maintains the setting has to be recreated at every session. Recreating and preserving is very different from automatically following the rules or re-establishing it after rules have been transgressed. The creation of the setting, which is the first phase of the therapy, is not only about dictating the methods and rules to be followed, but also about the patient's live emotional experience through which their co-operation in this process is engaged. We can see how the idea of the mirror-analyst is fading before the reality of two people reflecting together on the relationship: 'a couple engaged on a developmental task that is based on containing and transforming the emotional exchanges' (Zavattini, 1988).

The internal setting and the 'couple state of mind'

It is necessary to be precise about the specific mental orientation required for work with couples: that is, to be suitable for containing both the respective partners and their relationship. To recapitulate what has been described in previous chapters: Dicks' (1967) hypothesis of 'unconscious fit' allows the therapist to envisage how the internal world of each partner fits with that of the other, so to work on promoting reciprocity (Vellotti &

Zavattini, 2008). According to Ruszczynksi & Fisher (1995) 'the relationship itself' is the patient, and the therapist is the guarantor of the dimension shared between the two partners.

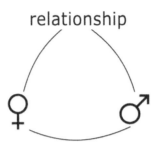

FIGURE I: The relationship as the third element

Particularly illuminating is Mary Morgan's (2001) useful concept of the 'couple state of mind'. This is a state which (as with Klein's 'positions') does not follow a rigidly linear course of either progression or regression, but fluctuates from one direction to another. Similar formulations are Colman's (1993) concept of 'marriage as psychological container'; Ruszczynksi's (2005) 'marital triangle'; and the creative relationship as described by Morgan & Ruszczynksi (1998). Morgan connects her own theory of the couple state of mind with Britton's (1989) 'third position', from which a more complex view of the relationship as a whole may be observed. This is the therapist's specific challenge. From the viewpoint of the 'couple state of mind' the therapist can empathise with each partner's position in an intimate relationship, whilst remaining sufficiently outside to reflect on the relationship itself. The couple state of mind is also the necessary condition in each partner for their relationship to function – to think as a unit whilst respecting their separateness. In some couples this may never have sufficiently developed; in others it may have become temporarily lost, as can happen in transitional or stressful times such as the birth of a child, adolescent changes, moving house, illness, or mourning – events that might put at risk a weak or insufficiently mature couple state of mind. So when this state of mind does not exist in the couple, it is the aim of the therapy to help try to establish and support it.

When couples come to therapy it is usually because they feel the lack of this third dimension, and they hope unconsciously that it may be found in the person of the therapist. They seek for a figure who is objective and who can help the partners to see each other and, at the same time, represent the relationship itself. It is very important in the evaluation of a couple if the idea of 'us' is present, as something added to each of their subjectivities, and to note whether this is felt to be an enrichment or a threat to the individuals. There are other couples, such as the following one, in which the idea of a couple does not exist; they demand of the therapist that he or she settle their arguments and it is very difficult to show that it is not just about arbitration. It is important to notice if what one person says is taken into account by the other, or if the capacity to listen is blocked off. For example a rationale on the lines of 'what she does' or 'what he does' indicates a linear causal link rather than a triangular or circular one, both of which acknowledge a wider system of causality in which all the elements modify or influence one another. The term 'circular causality' is derived from systems theory, and refers to the continual reciprocal influences between partners that affect the ground of all their relational transactions.

We will now look at the cases of two couples: one of them approaching a couple state of mind, and the other in whom it is absent.

Couple A

Mr and Mrs A got to know each other as teenagers. When they come to therapy they are 35 and 40 years old and have a child of seven. Mrs A says she asked for therapy because she wants to 'do anything that is possible to save their marriage in crisis'. Mr A says he resists the idea of psychological treatment but has come in order to please her. From these opening statements we see that for both, the relationship is present as a reality; the marriage is in crisis but they both believe it is possible to do something for it. It is the wife who proposes, but the husband accepts her proposal and follows her. They say that their difficulties arise because they can't agree on anything. They have found a method to not confront the problem: first they do what he proposes, then next time they do what she proposes. In this way they avoid confronting the real issues. Mr A hates discussions because they make him anxious. Mrs A feels him to be distant because they never discuss. She needs some response from him to feel she is part of his consideration. She would rather he criticised her so then the situation could be improved. The strategy they have adopted creates a precarious equilibrium in which they would like to find a meeting point but are not able to do so. So Mr and Mrs A are looking for a more than individualistic aspect in their relationship. Both of them understand that the relationship is a third entity and that they can contribute to make it work, but they both find it inaccessible. When they talk about one another they often use the word 'different'.

Couple B

The case of Mr and Mrs B is very different. They have much more difficulty in accessing a couple state of mind. They are middle-aged, have been married for 25 years, and have a teenage son. Their relationship after a series of difficulties has entered a state of crisis. They decided to separate, but after getting a legal separation they have nonetheless continued to live together for logistical reasons.

After a while Mrs B observed some signs in her husband that made her think of trying again; he agreed and thus they came to therapy. One thing that led to their separation was their son; he was a rebel and liked to disobey all their rules. Over him their differences regarding educational methods emerged. Mrs B explained the son was very aggressive toward her and she accused her husband of ignoring it. Mr B says this is not true, she is too rigid. They argue a lot about educational methods, criticising and blaming one another harshly. They cannot understand how the other does not agree with matters that to them appear obvious. Indeed they seem unable to believe that any opinion other than their own could even exist. Both appear disappointed in one another. When Mrs B used to recount the son's misdeeds not only did she feel misunderstood and unsupported by her husband but she also felt he did not even believe her. He felt offended because his wife used to assert that her father would never have permitted this kind of behaviour and therefore he felt humiliated. Both insist all their difficulties result from the other, and their happiness depends on the changes they desire.

This is an example of there being no 'couple state of mind'. They don't have the idea that the relationship is an entity in itself. They don't think in terms of circular causality, that is, that what they say influences the other and has an impact on the other's way of behaving. Their need for a guarantor, a third party, takes the form of looking for a judge. The sessions are invaded by aggressiveness and neither knows how to control their own. Mr B's aggression is not direct but is delegated to his son. The therapist feels she is expected to put order into this confused situation, contain all this aggression, whilst trying to reflect on the relationship and establish in herself a couple state of mind.

The couple state of mind is what helps the therapist to confront the pressures that induce collusion – as, for example, when one of the partners tries to give the therapist information that they are trying to keep secret from the other; this happens very frequently, but focussing on the setting, both psychological and formal, has a surprising effect on the couple, as it demonstrates the therapist's attempt not to collude with either party and his or her ability to keep within his mind a space for the other even whilst engaged with one (Morgan, 2001).

In the previous chapter describing the triangular space and how the relationship is built as a third entity alongside the two partners, we have seen how the healthy relationship can be represented by an equilateral triangle, an unbalanced relationship by a scalene triangle, and in some cases it can be considered a non-relationship (–R) and therefore be represented by an upside-down equilateral triangle. I would now like to point out some different ways in which the unbalanced (scalene) relationship may appear in clinical practice. It is by examining the countertransference that the therapist can ask himself to what extent he can maintain an equilateral state of mind, paying equal attention to both partners and to the relationship, or whether he cannot do this and therefore his transference becomes biased ('scalenised'). A slight bias during a session can be considered normal. In fact it is important for empathy that the therapist can be permeated by the projections and therefore lean towards one or other of the partners. This can happen in different ways. Some are easier to identify than others: for example, the subject of the session might lead one of the partners to talk more than the other; if this happens it is important to highlight with a comment what is happening. The scalenisation may happen in less objectifiable ways, more related to the countertransference. The therapist may sympathise with one more than the other, feel one is more credible than the other, or have difficulties with one or the other, or might be able to create hypothesis of the internal world, the reasons, and the objects that organise the internal world of one in particular. It is the partners themselves that create this imbalance, for example by trying to shift the attention of the therapist or by trying to make him feel he hasn't understood anything, marginalising him, or inducing the therapist to act, or to have specific desires that he wants fulfilled.

When these things happen it is important that the therapist ask himself if a scalene configuration is being created, if his mind has been captured by one of the partners. We believe these facts need to be read in terms of empathy which means in terms of communication and enable us to reflect on the state of mind and atmosphere of the session.

We will go back to Mr and Mrs B to illustrate the concepts of equilaterality and of scalenisation, adding some features of their personal history. The father of Mrs B is a strong man with strong emotions but also sexist and a bully. The mother of Mrs B is subjugated and Mrs B always thought she didn't want to be like her; although she had many quarrels with her father she always valued him. Her mother was so upset by the crisis in the daughter's marriage she even tried to kill herself. For a long time she was severely ill, in danger of death, and is even now bearing the consequences. It was at that point that Mrs B felt the husband still had some feelings towards here, and this was why she proposed to him that they try again; on the other hand she is very scared and does not want to put trust in him and then be disappointed again. Mr B has a brother two years younger than him; when he was born Mr B was sent to stay with his aunt.

During one session, Mrs B started again to give the reasons for her unhappiness: the husband always pretended not to see the behaviour of the son and she was not supported. Mr B again says it is not true, and that he simply felt her educational methods were mistaken. He blamed her for insisting too much, being too aggressive with the son, and says he had warned her that the boy wouldn't tolerate this. He related an episode that he believed showed the beginning of the breakdown between mother and son: one day whilst the son was 'chatting' on the computer she gave him a slap, and Mr B still remembers the son's scream.

The therapist feels shocked. She says he must have felt very scared by his wife's violent action. Mrs B changes the subject, and in a monotone she starts on the same recriminations. The therapist at this point sympathised with the husband; inside, she felt he was right, and realises she had internally scalenised, and she questions herself: is a personal comment towards one of the partners acceptable? It would be important that such a comment be balanced by a comment towards the other. This is why she tries to recover the situation by sympathising with the suffering of Mrs B; she addresses her saying it must be really difficult for her to think back on that episode. Mrs B says she had been so stressed that evening – she had gone out in the car, imagined she had bumped into something, and came back in a state not entirely normal. At this point we believe she is getting more in contact with her internal world, and the equilateral approach of the therapist allows her to keep both partners in mind and not collude with one of them.

In the session just depicted we can see how the re-balancing of equilateral behaviour on the part of the therapist after slight distortion has allowed Mrs B to develop her own reflective capacities.

We agree with Morgan (2001) who believes the couple state of mind is necessary even during brief consultations because it is the only containing factor that exists before the relationship with the therapist has formed. We suggest that the couple state of mind should continue throughout the therapy. The interpretations of the relationship that will be given later on (see the paragraph on joint interpretation) will be affected by the mental state of the therapist as he tries to understand what are the joint anxieties and unconscious phantasies.

The external setting

We have arrived now at what is usually referred to as the 'setting' but which we prefer to call 'external setting'. In couple therapy this will be in continuous dialogue with the internal setting of the therapist, namely his couple state of mind. Such a scenario can only be formed in the presence of a neutral external figure. Some of the variables integral to couple therapy are: stability; frequency and length of sessions; seeing the couple together; and the number of therapists.

Stability

We already know the reasons for stability in the individual therapy setting. In couple therapy too, the guarantee of regularity in the variables provides containment and an opportunity to talk about feelings. We also need to be aware that the development of a couple state of mind within our patients requires a lot of work, and in trying to achieve this one encounters many difficulties and resistances. For this reason the therapist will often have recourse to imposing a stricter type of setting than that in individual therapy, in order to enable the regulation of exchanges and reflections, as in the previous example.

In one session, after an initial prolonged silence, Mr B said with a lot of self-control that he didn't have anything important to say and it was just the usual things. After a while he became irritated, said he couldn't be bothered anymore, the therapy was useless, and he didn't want to live like this any more. All this because of a load of rubbish he left in a box! His wife had wanted him to apologise and admit his mistake in front of their son.

After this outburst he got up and asked the therapist to prepare the bill for next time. The therapist felt very disturbed and said she would wait for them. Meanwhile the wife too got up, grumbling.

The couple often test the therapist's patience in this way. A great effort of containment is needed to stop the situation from degenerating as it is here. One might think that in order to re-establish channels of communication, the therapist should have said 'I understand your need to deposit somewhere all the ugly stuff you have accumulated throughout the marriage, and you'd feel better if someone else took on the burden. However these problems will always be there if they are not confronted.' As mentioned earlier, argument between the couple during the session constitutes an attack on the analyst's ability to think: she therefore needs first to re-establish the possibility of communication, and then will be able to deal with the negative transference.

Frequency and length of sessions

Usually the frequency of sessions is weekly and the ideal length is 70–75 minutes, a time which is considered sufficient for both partners to express themselves but without accumulating more material than it is possible to discuss in one session.

In the model that we follow the 'here and now' and the matter of mental states and the emotions that circulate during the session are more important than attention to the internal worlds of one or other partner. There is less possibility of reaching the deep symbolic material than in individual therapy, because what is of prime importance is the concrete unfolding of relational facts during the session. Later we will go in more depth into how couple therapy finds its base in countertransference, moderate interpretation, and its gradual elaboration. The therapist's mental state differs from that of the classic listening position, since this could hinder the chance of allowing circularity (mutual influences) to arise within the equilaterality.

Joint sessions

We have already seen that in work conducted at the Tavistock Clinic, couples have in the past been dealt with separately, and only more recently has the joint session model been used by the Marital Studies Institute (now the Centre for Couple Relationships). In the early 1950s the joint session was considered risky and described by Balint as inducing an 'explosive situation'. Nevertheless Dicks experimented with joint couple sessions and described methods and objectives. The joint session allows us to confront in a more direct way the divisions between the couple and to reconstitute them. On top of that if there are two therapists they may be seen as co-therapist, meaning a couple that invites symbolisation at an unconscious level of the internal parental couple (Fisher, 1999). Fisher asserts it is important to give each partner the ability to unify in reality all their divisions and contradictions. Naturally the joint session does not determine this in itself, but we know that when all the split parts of the self are recognised and named, anxiety diminishes.

Moving to the practice of joint sessions also meant a shift in the theoretical model. We believe that this option allows us to understand contemporaneously the presence of both real partners, but also, their presence in the mind of the other, and the relationship itself, which is the real object of the therapeutical work.

Given this, it is an interesting question whether one always has to see the couple together. What would happen if the partners were seen separately, or if only one of them turned up to the session?

Couple C

Mr and Mrs C came to therapy at the suggestion of the therapist of their ten year old daughter (the girl has difficulty relating to her peers). Mrs C has a collaborative demeanour but very formal such that the therapist finds it essentially defensive and devaluing. Mr C seems bland and clumsy, talks little and stutters when he does speak. It was a great effort for them to come to talk about their marital crisis. They both had other relationships though at first they do not talk about these. In the past, Mr C had had a confrontation with his own mother when he had a relationship with a girl of whom she did not approve; he even thought of leaving home. At that point he had begun to confide in his present wife and slowly this relationship had taken over.

When their daughter was two she was the victim of an accident; though both parents were present they were unable to prevent it, and both felt guilty though there is no objective justification for this. There are now no lasting physical consequences but the trauma of the past event has endured. After it Mrs C fell into a light depression and became distanced from her husband. She locked herself in her room and cried; Mr C did not understand what was going on and started to confide in a female colleague. So we have Mr C as an 'absent' father, and Mrs C as an efficient and domineering mother. When they speak of the girl's school, Mrs C criticises the teachers, holding as a model in her head the example of her mother who was a teacher, always very busy preparing lessons and always showing her own daughter what she was going to do in class. Mrs C, trapped by her picture of a narcissistic faultless attentive mother, is oppressed by the idea that she was not sufficiently alert with her own daughter, and seems persecuted by this hypercritical internal object. Mr C, who has difficulties with this type of female figure, turns to another type, escaping into an adolescent mental state very far from that of a couple: threatening to leave, attacking the relationship searching indirectly for revenge. As much as Mrs C shifts towards parenthood, Mr C shifts to childish attitudes and behaviour.

At the fourth meeting, after the therapist had said she was prepared to offer therapy to the couple, though had not yet explained all the aspects of the setting including that of the joint session, Mr C arrived for the appointment, more lively than usual. He says his wife is not very well, has flu, and it is better to have some sessions by himself so the therapist can understand certain things better. He can't say everything while his wife is present. He also thinks the wife might need this type of session. Unexpectedly he starts to talk incessantly, first about the relationship with the colleague – which never turned into an affair – and now they are just friends. However there had been other women 'even a little harem' as he puts it, and he talks about them in a scattered way for a long time, 'like a teenager' he says; he talks of confidences, intimacy, attraction, but not actually sexual consummation. His wife had been very jealous of some of these women.

With this couple, we are faced with an unconscious agreement that Mr C always uses the same mechanism: when he has difficulty with a woman (the first girlfriend, the ill wife) he substitutes by finding another – the colleague, the therapist. If this is Mr C's way of attacking the couple relationship, Mrs C does it by falling ill, undermining the proposition of therapy by removing herself from it. Mrs C is involved in the triad of mother, herself, daughter; this is why she desexualises herself and removes herself from the couple relationship. Mr C tries to re-involve her but through provocation. He tries to re-sexualise her by means of arousing jealousy. He attacks the therapy as well, by trapping the therapist in a secret confidence that unbalances the equilateral setting because this means there is an a certain psychic reality shared between them that the therapist cannot use.

In order to defend the therapeutical project and not collude with the patients' attempts to distract it, we think it is best to avoid having sessions with only one partner. If only one arrives, it is a good idea to sit them down, apologise about not having been clear about the working method, explain why the session is joint, then send them away. Only later can one see how to get to interpret these negative aspects of their unconscious fit. In the first instance it is necessary not to collude in attempts to undermine the therapeutic dynamics, and instead to redirect focus towards the couple relationship as an entity.

One or two therapists?

Both options are possible; but they build two different scenarios. The two-therapist option is particularly complex because many relationships intertwine: the transference between the members of the couple, and that to the therapists, which will deepen. The therapists will have to be aware of all these inter-relationships. The two therapists need to be able to work well together, discuss each session afterwards, confront reciprocal feelings, analysing their respective countertransference; at the same time it allows them to explore better the multiple aspects of the couple relationship via the game of identification and criss-crossed transferences. The variable that is linked to the gender of the therapists is significant, because it affects identification, alliances, sense of exclusion, and highlights more the dynamics between the partners; and of course it has a heavier role when there are two therapists, so it is best if one therapist is male and the other female. Various different situations can emerge and manifest themselves. A patient for example may seek an alliance with the therapist of the same gender, seeking for support through gender identity. Another may seek an alliance with the therapist of the opposite sex, relying on an oedipal situation. Or the two partners can create a solidarity between them in a kind of teenage opposition to the couple of parental therapists. All this may allow the therapists to understand better the patients and their couple organisation.

The transference

The literature on couple psychoanalytical psychology which has stressed that the fit between internal worlds can be considered a type of natural transference refers tot eh gheory of object relations (D. & J. Scharff, 1991; Ruszczynski & Fisher, 1995; Fisher, 1999). From these studies one deduces that the transference between the members of the couple is a crucial and particularly complex matter with which the therapist has to deal.

This requires a big shift from work with individuals. While the individual patient brings to the session a representation of their partner, and of themselves in relation to the partner, these two dimensions slowly slide into the transference relationship with the therapist.

The couple also brings their couple transference. So there are two types of transference: the couple transference (the unconscious fit between partners) and the transference onto the therapist or therapist-couple that emerges during the session.

To understand this it is helpful to envisage a vertical dimension (the organisation of each partner's internal world) and a horizontal dimension (how the expectations of one fit with the expectations of the other). As we saw in Chapter 2, in their choice of partner, each seeks to match their own internal world; this is what constitutes the couple transference. Understanding the couple transference therefore means to have a working hypothesis not only of the relationship but also of its responsiveness, meaning, how the internal world of one partner tunes into and makes contact with the internal world of the other. The therapist's couple state of mind involves thinking in terms of circular rather than linear causality. It is different from individual therapy and allows him to confront the partners' couple transference.

The Scharffs (1991) refer to the differences that Winnicott describes between mother–environment and mother–object; they talk about 'contextual transference' as a sustaining structure, and about 'focal transference' to that particular therapist – the latter being what Norsa & Zavattini (1997) call 'differentiated transference'. The contextual transference aroused by the setting is the response of the patients to the encounter with the therapist, a person offering help, and has to do with availability more than with unconscious resistance. The focal transference concerns the relationship with that particular therapist. Both types of transference include trust, idealisation, hopes, fears, and distrust. They can be harmonious when the partners share the same feeling, or disturbed when the partners have different feelings.

One also needs to specify that within the transference to the therapist will be found both the individual transference from each partner, and the transference that they place on it as a couple, in relation to the function of the therapist as a shared object (Eiguer, 1996). In this case each partner can be a carrier of one of the different aspects of the transference especially when this is imbued with ambivalence (Monguzzi, 2010). In fact the couple becomes a unified psychic organisation, an intermediate space between the partners for shared phantasies, feelings, needs, defences, and they redistribute all these mental contents through their reciprocal projective identifications.

It can happen therefore that if two aspects of the couple's psychic organisation are in conflict, one becomes the prerogative of one of the partners, and the other, the prerogative of the other partner. The two partners become representatives of two different aspects of their unconscious fit or collusion.

The transference to the therapist can include some very entan-gled intertwinings. Norsa and Zavattini (1997) have referred to dyads and triads of possible collusions, and to configurations in which one or both therapists are cut out of the conversation, or one of the two partners is marginalised.

The concept of 'field' comes in here, being the way in which the organisation of the couple makes contact with the organ-isation of the setting constructed by the therapist and there-fore with the therapist's couple mental state of mind. Bezoari and Ferro (1991) have proposed the oscillatory nature of the transference relationship. In a new experience the transference does not merely repeat predetermined patterns induced by unconscious phantasies and projective identification. The field approach amplifies the psychoanalytic perspective from a study of contents to a study of the transformational potential of the analytical environment. In the session, the therapist listens to the various interventions, reflects on his own, and asks what is the general direction and what underlying psychoanalytical object is organising the exchanges between the participants. Post-Bionian authors such as Ferro and Ogden see the characters who are described in the session neither as realistic ones from the past, nor solely as internal objects or part-objects, but as created by the dreamlike contact between the analyst and analysand – the latter, in the case of couple therapy, being the relationship between the partners.

In synthesis: during the session the couple transference and the transference to the therapist intertwine continuously. The therapist needs to distinguish them only for clarity. The couple psychotherapist does not work solely with the couple transfer-ence which is always a construction; he works rather with the way this mixes with the transference to the therapist, and with their present relationship with him. He needs to ask himself how each partner reacts to the first psychoanalytic object that emerges, and how he himself feels in his countertransference, so he can understand what is the dominant feature of the session, its 'atmosphere', organising all its phenomenology. Hypotheses are constructed not only about the individuals' internal worlds and their interaction, but about the dynamics of the new field that is created by the meeting of their couple 'organiser' and the setting given by the analyst.

To illustrate how the couple transference onto the therapist may manifest itself, I will return to the example of Couple A.

A short while into the course of the therapy, a very difficult question for them to confront emerges. Mrs A talks about how he masturbates; he has always done it, but now she can't stand it any more. Before, she thought it was her fault and she was not sufficiently sexually available; then she though this was not the case because he assured her she had nothing to do with it. Mr A says everyone does it and it has nothing to do with their relationship and he doesn't understand why it disturbs her so much.

So we can see how here is a situation in which the woman does not feel acknowledged by the husband and feels neglected, while the husband feels controlled by her. We know from their personal histories that they both had a difficult relationship with their own mothers. Mrs A was born a year after the death of a little sister. Her life's experience was that of feeling a substitute child, always filling the vacuum. She never felt loved by her mother who always remembered with nostalgia and regret the perfection of the other daughter. Mr A has an authoritarian and controlling mother which he suffered; as a teenager he rebelled but there were terrible quarrels, after which his mother would not speak to him for days on end. She was jealous of the girls with whom he had relationships. Both fathers (of Mr and Mrs A) left the protagonist's role to their wives and leaned on them.

Both Mr and Mrs A relive in their couple relationship the bad relationship with their mothers. Mrs A finds it in the husband's masturbation and lack of interest in her and feels mortified. Mr A projects on the wife a controlling figure and his masturbation signifies his assertion of his autonomy, to extract himself from domination and redeem his independence. Both would like their partner to offer them a different experience from one which they are unable to work through and which leaves them feeling wounded and powerless. Mrs A would like to feel interest and appreciation; Mr A would like to feel respected in his autonomy. This is what their couple transference consists of, which also determines their unconscious fit.

At one session, they arrive punctually and are immediately invited into the room. Mr A says, 'You don't even let us go to the toilet.' From this we see how Mr A projects onto the therapist the controlling figure of his mother, against whom he feels the need to retaliate, in order to carve an intimate and private space. He fears the therapist might prevent this (she does not allow him to go to the toilet) and he wants to assert the legitimacy of his need. We notice also that he speaks in the plural ('us'). He involves the wife, asking her to be his ally and to leave this authoritarian figure outside the couple. This happened even more clearly at another time. One day the therapist heard them laughing in the waiting room. When they enter, happy and relaxed, they say they were asking themselves what homework they were supposed to do: 'Well they haven't done it!' The therapist observes how they find togetherness and complicity, happiness, only when in a teenage frame of mind: having projected onto her the role of authority figure, they feel liberated. For the therapist it is therefore necessary to live with a relationship in which, although accepting the role given her of castrating and mortifying maternal figure, she somehow has to transform the role into one that is encouraging and appreciative.

Interpretations and other interventions

The therapeutic work with couples can include interventions at various levels. Some may be more direct, to facilitate and maintain the logic of the setting, as described above. Or there may be interpretations on deeper aspects. Interpretations themselves should be divided into those which are about the needs, relations, internal objects of one or other of the partners; and those that refer to the joint phantasy logic of the couple in terms of their unconscious fit or collusion.

The transformative function of the setting

As we have seen, the joint setting creates a shared physical and mental space for the couple's relationship in the presence of a therapist with a couple state of mind and equilateral mental aspect. All this creates a containment that makes thinkable and communicable the emotions that are aroused. At first, and for a while, the therapist will limit him or herself to guaranteeing this setting, taking care of the marital triangle created by the couple and their relationship (Ruszczynski, 2005).

In the case of Mr and Mrs B, for example: this couple came to therapy after a legal separation. They had therefore tried with a judge and court to find a container for their emotional emergency and to find an intermediary who could give some guarantee of protection from which they could tackle and resolve their mutual aggressiveness. For couples like this with a really disturbed relationship with sparse means of working through it, and with whom it is not possible to reach high levels of symbolisation, it is necessary to confront the most primal toxic contents. In such cases it is already a big achievement to re-establish equilaterality, a non-biased perspective, and to draw attention to circularity, to mutual causation.

Confrontation or comment

Demonstrating circularity of behaviour is the first stage in therapy, and the only one possible in cases such as this. To interpret more directly any feature of either partner's internal world may be too precocious an approach to the intersubjective aspect underlying the interaction. Often the therapist's function is to regulate the conversation so they contribute in turns, even if (as we have seen) it means that he needs to be more directorial and take charge of the orchestration of the shared space. He allows both partners to express their own rationale, and creates a context for better communication. In theoretical terms, this type of structure emphasises the function of containment, facilitating the development of premises for a reflective function (Allen & Fonagy, 2006). Fundamental milestones for this development are: the ability to observe the effect of one's own behaviour and subjectivity on the other, and observation of the circularity of actions with their opposing reactions. This helps the growth of a capacity to look from the outside at what is happening within the relationship. It favours the highest level of symbolisation possible at that moment for that couple.

Interpretation

The question of interpretation, even before being a matter of technique, is a matter of how one sees the nature of interpretation. This is what inspires us to read in a particular way the quality of the exchanges in the session and then to adopt an appropriate technique.

To recapitulate: the classic or reconstructive view of interpretation sees unconscious fit as the meeting point of two fixations or unresolved elements from the past that re-emerge in the present. It is also the theory most commonly used (Castellano, Velotti, & Zavattini, 2010; Zavattini, 2010). The other traditional view, followed especially in the 1960s and 1970s, considers that concord may fail owing to disappointment when one partner does not match up to an idealised projection of the other's own personal history, or finds themselves the receptacle of a rejected part of the self projected into them, not at an intrapsychic level but at an interpersonal level. Both these lines of interpretation are limited by being reconstructive: the present unconscious fit occurs as a result of unresolved elements from the past.

In the intersubjective model, unconscious fit is not fully explained by history but depends on the 'here and now' of the present relationship. As Bowlby (1988) said, the modes of internal operation constructed by childhood history are reprocessed throughout life, especially in less pathological situations, not just in infancy but through adolescence, and not just with other caregivers (parents, teachers, family) but with other significant relationships. We believe that in fact everyone uses their relationships with others to re-set their internal organisation, and that the individual's present mode of internal operation is based partly on past history and partly on the present. Memory is not archival as Freud thought but is continually reprocessed with each new experience (Zavattini, Pace, Santona, 2010).

So a couple that comes to therapy is at least partially aware that their project is in crisis and they have not been able to resolve sufficiently the defects of their personal history. Their previous significant relationships can be considered as testing grounds but each relationship is different, including that of the therapy. From the therapist's point of view, having an interest in what each patient has learned from each relationship helps to access the script which is created from the encounter of two internal worlds but does not explain completely the present meaning of the relationship (Velotti & Zavattini, 2008).

Further, Rudzinsky's proposal that the patient is the relationship itself rather than either or both of the individuals involved (Rudzinsky & Fisher, 1995) brings out the vertical and horizontal dimensions of this interpretative model (see figure below). The horizontal dimension represents the organisation of the self within the couple – how the internal of one fits with the internal world of the other. Norsa and Zavattini (1997), following this model, have distinguished between 'differentiating interpretations' and 'joint interpretation'. Differentiating interpretations refer to the part-identifications of each partner and risk reducing the problems to influences from the past. Joint interpretations, discussed below, focus on the relationship as it presents itself in the session.

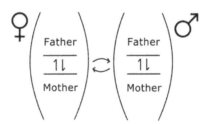

FIGURE 2: Vertical and horizontal dimensions

Essentially when one positions the relationship as the object of interpretation, one can investigate the collusion and the shared aspects, but without sacrificing the more individual aspects. The interpretation should privilege the horizontal but not exclude the vertical, that is, what one is projecting onto the other. Thus there should never be any session where only one partner is present as this would not favour circularity and equilaterality.

Joint interpretations

This method consists in seeking for the couple's 'organising theme' or 'shared internal object' (Norsa & Zavattini, 1997). Being together produces a new reality and a new subject, the relationship itself, which becomes the patient. The field model is relevant here. As in individual therapy, in couple therapy the aim is to mobilise the field and as a consequence to reactivate the paralysed projective and introjective processes which lie behind the suffering (Neri, 2007). This experience allows the circulation of emotional states, affections, thoughts, and characters, with the analyst who is also in the field, and who guarantees and safeguards the setting; this promotes a thinking activity in both patients and therapist.

For all the analyst's perceptions can be communicated either as observations or, through reverie, transformed into images or narratives (Ferro, 2005). The latter may be considered as being in a sense beyond interpretation, but rather, show the analyst as a dynamic element in the space built by identifications between characters.

According to Ferro (2006, 2007, 2020) the analytical journey offers a space in which whatever the analytical couple brings to it finds welcome. Development happens through micro-experiences of being on the same wavelength rather than by decodifying interpretations. The function is to create a new transformative relation. Ferro talks of 'co-narrative transformation', dialogic co-operation, referring to the way in which the therapist engages with the patient's discourse rather than simply commenting on it from outside. Excessive precision and detail may block the process.

However many couples in fact bring to the session very mundane concerns, so that even before thinking of a transformative therapeutic relationship, we have to think of an earlier phase in which a container is formed which can confront evacuative necessities, tolerate tensions and excesses, and allow the experience of a welcoming space (Bolognini, 2008). As in individual therapeutic work, containment is expressed first of all by sharing the meaning that appears in the patient's communication. The fact of being able to perceive and share the meaning leads to more trustful communications with the therapist. In couple therapy this occurs through the equilateral receptive function, which means conflict within the relationship may diminish and reflective capacity may be increased.

We can imagine the couple as an ensemble in which in some cases the splitting and projection allots to each partner an aspect of the couple's mental functioning. No matter who expresses it, the couple can evacuate in this way emotions which are uncontainable, in the form of acting out (Santona & Zavattini, 2008). As previously suggested, one of the reasons for doing joint couple therapy is to confront differences: to try to rebalance the splitting through which each person is glued to just one point of view. In this way emotional communication will be re-established, split parts will be reappropriated, and ambivalence and contradictions will be confronted. What one sees all the time is the therapist containing primitive or split emotions that are felt to be too aggressive or dangerous for the relationship to acknowledge. When the relationship disappoints this expectation of containment, the therapy then becomes the place that offers an opportunity to receive unwanted emotions; this is necessary for transformation.

Mr and Mrs C, whom we talked about earlier, argue about the mess in their house. They relate this in a strongly contrasting yet collusive manner. Mrs C has not yet unpacked boxes from their move to that house, and in addition is always making new purchases in the hope of renovating but is unable to get rid of anything. Mr C too is always buying abundant quantities of various items and in order to clear up he seals everything in plastic bags that he accumulates in piles. They both forget what they have put away and where, and both seem unable to use the gadgets they have acquired, and ask the therapist to convince the other to change their ways. The therapist thinks about the difficulty of understanding emotional experiences that have accumulated in a messy way and which they cannot transform, like the objects in the house. If they both have difficulty in putting things in order, and experience each other as an invasion in their personal sphere, they at the same time find an accomplice in each other in the process of making the house unlivable in so they are unable to enjoy the things that they have.

In the preceding session, the therapist had a sudden emergency and was unable to let the patients know as they had already left. When she phoned in the evening, Mrs C was glad to hear from her as she had been worried. She said they had not gone to the session because they had forgotten. She said 'actually they had even forgotten to take their child to her therapist, and this is even worse!' In the next session, they again blamed each other for the messy accumulation of objects that they buy. Mrs C understands it all needs to be put in order, but she has to re-examine each object one by one, but Mr C refuses to help her because he sees this method as too time-consuming. He thinks everything should just be thrown away and complains there are hundreds of boxes. Mrs C says the boxes are hers, but the plastic bags are his.

They continue this exchange of accusations, while the therapist reflects these inanimate characters that are so burdensome and yet nameless are impossible to deal with. She also thinks about her own function as a form of environment officer, who tries to declutter and create boundaries of thought in which names can be given to confused and unrecognised emotions. At this point she stops them by saying that what they want her to do is to be a referee in a situation they find confusing; each attributes to the other things that they cannot recognise in themselves. Maybe what they are saying is that they feel they have cluttering emotional experiences, with which they have difficulty and which they cannot reorganise. They need to understand what is whose. They feel invaded by each others' boxes and bags. In the face of the burden and effort and time-consumption of this reordering work, they would just prefer to throw everything away. However if one just eliminates things, one has the sensation of losing something important from one's self.

ls that it is easier to order more recent stuff,
ers what is in the containers. Amongst all the
bilities the therapist chose to focus on that
the joint interpretation of unconscious fit,
Mr and Mrs C have assigned her. However
to dig for deeper symbolic material is not
accepted; Mr and Mrs C find it hard to understand the symbol-
ism of their boxes and bags.

The therapist tries to stay within the here and now of the
field, acknowledging Mrs C's last observation. She asks, what
have they done with what they felt the previous week when
they did not find her at the session at their appointment. She
observes that because they don't talk about it, maybe they have
closed this episode in a box or a bag. Mrs C responds promptly,
shifting the discussion onto her own forgetfulness, referring to
the time when they forgot to take their daughter to her analyst.
After that however she declares she was very worried, since
usually the therapist is very precise and she must have had a
setback; she even starts to talk about the possibility of an accident. The therapist says maybe the thought of an accident was
too much, so at first she just thought of a setback. But another
thought was more painful: that she might have forgotten. She
talks of her own forgetfulness, but maybe is thinking that even
the therapist might have forgotten. Mrs C acknowledges this.
But then she felt relieved, thinking it was not so bad and the
therapist was human and could also make a mistake. Mr C says
he did not believe the therapist could have forgotten, he only
imagined an accident and that perhaps she was dead, as she had
not even phoned. But when she phoned he was relieved so he no
longer thought about it. The therapist observes that it would be
ideal if everything could be resolved like this: just a phone call
and there's an end to it. Even the resentment that the therapist
had not even phoned had disappeared (unacknowledged). In
fact however, only had she been dead would they really have
accepted it. (They all laugh even to crying.)

Mrs C said in fact she had managed to get rid of some stuff,
and had put some still new items in boxes for a charity fair run
by a relative. She felt happy as it was true she felt the need to

revitalise things; the relief was so strong one did feel like crying. That time she had the help of her aunt. She needed the help of her husband. Mr C replies that he is trying to do something to help her. After the therapist with her joke demonstrated she was able to accept their anxiety, the atmosphere became lighter and something new appeared in the field. Mr and Mrs C passed from mundane realities to something closer to symbolic narrative, which was liberating. The therapist had not thrown away the contents of the box and the emotions could be confronted. Mr and Mrs C had been trying to use one another as container, blaming one other for not being good enough for that function. They are invaded by strong emotions that they cannot process, and the temptation to use one another to evacuate these emotions has failed. Only the experience of a large, solid, but flexible container (the therapist) is able to offload the emotional weight without rancour towards their partner, allowing them to think that they can perform this decluttering and recycling operation with the help of the therapist who is not afraid to get her hands dirty. The final statements of Mr and Mrs C indicate that they can foresee this possibility at last.

Conclusion

This chapter has considered theory and techniques in the development of couple therapy: concluding in particular that it needs to be based on a specific state of mind in the therapist, the couple state of mind. This triangular space is what allows the patients, following the example of the therapist, to feel part of the relationship yet observe it from outside.

In the studies in this book we find most useful models which encourage the therapy to move forward experientially in the field created by the participants, rather than solely unravelling the past of individual partners, as projected into their choice of partner in mutual collusion. The focus is on the 'here and now' and on the demands of 'welcoming' and understanding the emotions circulating throughout the session. Interpretation in the traditional sense is only one of the tools available in conducting the session, and is used sparingly. Every communication made during the session is in fact relevant to the therapeutical dynamic. Couple therapy practiced in this way has shifted from a reconstructive to a constructive model of the process, in which the relationship between patient(s) and therapist(s) is an interactive one. As we shall see in the next chapter, emotional patterns and positions that are implicit but not fully known can be brought into being within the therapy and new developmental scenarios can be envisaged.

CHAPTER FIVE

Couple psychoanalysis and intersubjectivity

Fabio Monguzzi

'*Nemo solus satis sapit* [No single person knows enough]'
(Plautus, *Miles Gloriosus,* 885)

This chapter is by way of conclusion and theoretical summary of our approach to couple therapy as described in this book, based as it is on developments in the current psychoanalytical landscape that combine the relational paradigm (as described by Mitchell, 1988, 2000) with the intersubjective paradigm (Stolorow & Atwood, 1992; Stolorow *et al.,* 1994), and that has been defined by some as 'postmodern' (Fallone, 2004): that is, that values relativity, context, the co-existence of different truths, and takes a non-linear view of progress. This landscape is a fertile one but seems to have been developed more in individual psychotherapy than in work with couples, where as we have said, the real patient is the relationship between the partners.

Because couple therapy specifically manages the unified psychic processes of both partners, we consider it not merely a format but a genre with its own distinctive characteristics. The intersubjective school of thought facilitates the definition of these characteristics, since it focuses on the reciprocal influence of patient and analyst, and legitimises the role of the analyst in becoming one of the determinants of psychic change between the two. It prioritises the increase of containment abilities, more than the attempt to reintegrate split-off emotions. Couple therapy based solely on object relations looks at the psychic complementarity of the partners, their shared internal objects, and communal phantasies crisscrossing a network of projections and identifications. The aim is to release the grip of these intrusive processes, to reintegrate emotions, and to achieve adequate psychic separation between the partners (Scharff & Scharff, 1991; Ruszczynski, 1993; Ruszczynski & Fisher, 1995; Norsa & Zavattini, 1997; Corigliano, 1999). Couple therapy that embraces an intersubjective model emphasises the management, regulation, and balancing of feelings, holding them on behalf of each partner, known as hetero-regulation; it pays less attention to the degree of separateness and autonomy which is offered by a stable recognition of the boundaries of self and other (Shaddoc, 2000). In addition to acknowledging the relevance of problems from the past, the transformative potential of the here and now is given particular value.

Regulation of emotions within the couple relationship

The recent theoretical models for couple therapy have been influenced by research in the field of child development and interpersonal relationships. The couple relationship is the emotional bond most close to childhood relationships, configuring itself as a new caregiving environment. Early interactive processes between caretaker and infant are the basis for self–other regulation and for (mutual) hetero-regulation within couple relationships (Beebe & Lachmann, 2002; Clulow, 2007). This important paradigm for understanding adult relationships supposes that partners should be able to regulate emotional proximity and distance, and manage moments of loss of contact that occur owing to incomprehension or splits; they can create reparational strategies to reintroduce harmony and enable continuation of the relationship (Carli, Cavanna, & Zavattini, 2009). For the sense of emotional proximity and intimacy partners can experience seems deeply correlated to functions and mechanisms that regulate reciprocity in childhood caregiving. The qualities and nature of dependency, the oscillation between belonging and separation, the negotiation of differences, all have their first investigations in this developmental period.

Thus when interpreting a couple's difficulties in connecting with one another we need to analyse their emotional understanding and attunement and the quality of reciprocity in the containment they can offer. We need to put the analysis first in the sense of being a space where mutual regulation can create an equilibrium that facilitates developmental processes. In this space emotional disconnections and unregulated dyadic states will appear that have ignited situations of crisis in the past. These are features not of the individual partners and their personal ability to symbolise their phantasies but of the relationship itself, which stimulates new directions and also new problems. The encounter between individual characteristics does not only bring up new editions of existing models that were developed in the primal relationships, but also creates new experiences, since the relationship is subject to the usual changes and vicissitudes of life.

We find that often one of the partners initiates and supports the transformation whilst the other embodies the fears and anxieties: 'You are pushing me to become something I can't.' Each person's potentialities and predispositions find expression in a shared process of becoming, on different levels and in different ways (Monguzzi, 2010). Their individual past histories are a necessary condition but not sufficient for understanding the current couple relationship. New relational modes will also have been acquired through their experiences as a couple in the near past, leading to better or worse forms of linkage (Castellano, Velotti & Zavattini, 2010).

As shown in previous chapters we can see that the couple relationship acts as itself a psychic container (Colman, 2003) so the containment is not created only by alternating balanced reciprocity between each partner. The outcome of the union is seen as a process of creation to be supported, arousing aspirations for its identity, not just desire for containment (Zavattini, 2006). It is important that the partners understand that it is in this psychic space with its aspirations to expansion and reparation that the therapist will invest his efforts, attempting to heal the narcissistic wound that has broken out as a result of the crisis between them and to restore a positive gaze between one and the other (Lemaire, 1979).

Having a sufficiently complex view of the relationship guarantees a level of psychic functioning where a different or even opposite perspective in the other is not seen as invalidating one's own, but can be tolerated and kept in mind so it can enter in dialogue with one's own thoughts and emotions. If these conditions exist, one feels the relationship may survive the arguments, in hope that there can be reciprocal understanding even where there is a difference of opinion. The relationship can be experienced as a resource, a mental space for objectively observing the orientation of each individual. This position allows the relationship in its entirety to be thought about, not just its separate components. If such a space does not exist, the strength of the emotions in play between the partners becomes overwhelming and a primitive state of mind inimical to mentalisation (Allen & Fonagy, 2006) may set in, characterised by positions of attack and defence; the reflective function that endows one's own and others' feelings with meaning has been incapacitated.

For many couples the determining agent in therapy is not only the specific response to their own problems, but the presence of the therapist as a responsive subject, whose responsive mental states seem to offer a mirror for their own. The informative role of words is less important than their function as revealing mental states (Steiner, 1993). The 'what' of the experience prevails over the 'why' (Monguzzi, 2010). In these situations it seems that containment has priority over the need to understand specific interpretations. The therapist's participatory role in the here and now of the session offers a perspective through which expectations and roles can be renegotiated (Bromberg 1998).

From the intersubjective perspective, we consider the processes that engage and interest the partners and the therapist reciprocally, in the field that exists between them, rather than how phantasies and defences operate in the individual worlds of the partners. The therapist himself is part of this field: considering not only the phantasy life of the couple but how it is organised in relation to himself and to the world. The emotional aspect of the present situation has more importance than the unresolved knots of the past, even though they still play a role in generating the difficulties that emerge into view. We consider the way discourse is articulated, and the dynamics of reciprocal influence. One partner's story always includes some emotional reflexes of the other. In a situation where one thing leads to another, each partner can learn to recognise themselves in the other's narrative. Both doubts and confirmations keep the discourse rolling rather than interrupting it. A new form with a shared thread of meaning can shape itself.

The premise of the intersubjective approach is that the therapist can know only when he contributes to creating. What impact will all these complex resonances have on the mind of the therapist? He will bring his own associations, thoughts and phantasies, and be more attuned to some themes than others, either consciously or unconsciously. Which pathways will he choose to pursue and which to bypass? These are the sorts of questions we ask ourselves. The therapist has to be careful in his countertransference, since not only his explicit behaviour but also his implicit mentalisations have considerable influence on the transferential field between the participants (Zucconi, 2004).

Silvia and Giovanni – working towards intersubjectivity

I shall now describe some of the problems encountered in working towards intersubjectivity, with the help of vignettes from work with one couple, Silvia and Giovanni.

In the first scenario, at the start of the treatment, Silvia phones to arrange a first consultation together with her husband. A few days later her husband Giovanni rings to try to change the date of the appointment. I phone him the same day and get no answer, so leave a message on the machine giving my availability and adding that I will be reachable on the phone for the next few hours, otherwise we could speak the next morning. I get no answer. On the day of the original appointment Silvia calls me in a hurry asking for the address of the consulting room, without mentioning her husband's phonecall.

When I meet them in the waiting room I am surprised to meet a terse and gloomy woman who seems very different from the one on the phone, and a man with a very paranoid demeanour. Once they are seated comfortably I briefly mention the phone communications and am immediately interrupted by Giovanni who says peremptorily that he has never received any messages from me. I say I am sorry to hear this and tell them the content of the message I left. He looks at me in a threatening way and says that if I had left a message he would have received it because his phone is a very reliable worktool.

In the following minutes other elements emerge. I learn that Silvia perceives her husband as excessively controlling, and it arouses her resentment. She says she is exasperated by Giovanni telling her all the time she is inadequate. Giovanni says his wife is indifferent, not interested in him, engaged only in her own activities, work, friendships, and children; he feels excluded and this provokes aggressive reactions and sometimes violence.

Witnessing all this, I wonder what interpretive level I should be using. Should I analyse the circuit of high emotional resonance which emerges, asking what are the meanings of Silvia's need for autonomy – what projected movements are happening and therefore what does the husband represent for her at this moment in time. I could also ask where, for Giovanni, do the feelings of exclusion come from – what past patterns are called up to take shape in the present context. These are the questions posed by a historical reconstructive point of view, where what happens in the session in the couple's interactions is given meaning in terms of reliving the past in the present. The stories and beliefs that unfold in the transference and countertransference set off associations through phrase and phantasy, in the form of analogies and differentiations. However following this associative approach exclusively, with its research into wider connections of the individual partners, might detract from concentrating on the present experience.

From an intersubjective perspective, I had to consider not only projections that may be in operation but also what in my own behaviour and attitude had contributed to creating the phenomena observed. Could the resentment and rage of the partners could be linked to feelings of inadequacy sparked by my not being able to answer their request (the phonecall) and also to their not being able to make contact in a convenient or appropriate way, both in the time of the appointment, and in locating the consulting room. Speaking to Giovanni, I said it was a real pity we were not able to speak on the phone and agree on a more convenient time. I added also that I asked why we had not been able to speak and that maybe it was because it was not after all necessary to change the time. Silvia, after listening in silence, said the matter of the appointment caused a quarrel between them: Giovanni had been upset, saying that she had fixed it after consulting only her own timetable and not his, but, she says, this is not true. Then Giovanni, in a resentful tone, says she always does what she wants without considering his needs, thinking he is always available. What I tried to do therefore was to empathise with the patients' more vulnerable and disturbing emotions, their rage and disappointment, to help regulate the emerging state of mind, and avoid letting the confusion impede the intersubjective exploration (Hughes 2007).

Negotiating the therapeutic climate

In recent years much attention has shifted onto non-interpretive factors in creating change, in particular onto the relationship as a vehicle for therapeutic action. The concept of negotiating the therapeutic climate refers to a wellknown article of Gabbard and Westen (2003) in which they address the subject of multiple modes of therapeutic action and the strategies for fostering therapeutic change. They stress the need for synergy between the modes available. These include: fostering insight, the nature of reciprocity, and viewing the relationship itself as a vehicle of therapeutic action.

Authors on intersubjectivity (Stolorow, Atwood, Lachmann, Orange) hold that the patient involves the therapist in a relationship in which his participation in the process of co-constructing the intersubjective experience, which becomes the object of 'negotiation' or exploration, is evident. The therapist therefore becomes drawn in to a 'minimal level of collusion' (Carli, 1993). He intentionally yields in order to participate emotionally through the only interactive mode which seems possible. The transformational aspect then lies in the possibility that a negotiation takes place in which the therapist, although apparently adhering to the relational suppositions of the patient, also distances himself, in order to suggest a new mode of interacting from within that position, and to expand the repertoire of emotional possibilities that are available. What is being negotiated are the meanings of the mutual experiences, the quality of the emotional participation, the interactive configurations, the ongoing construction of the therapeutic narrative (Albasi, 2007). The therapist's engagement in this process can be an important therapeutic factor because he is seen as a figure who is available to become involved in the intersubjective field; from this position he can actively propose a new experience that can then be memorised as an alternative relational proposition to the ones already known. The negotiation of the therapeutic environment therefore entails the involvement of a shared experiential dimension, at a level of implicit interaction that then becomes explicit, in which the aim is to find functional modes of affect regulation.

The consultation with Silvia and Giovanni that began so brusquely with the quarrel over the date of the appointment continued with them speaking of their jobs. Giovanni says: 'She manages a business; I sell, sell, sell.' Silvia in turn explains how in her business, no-one takes responsibility for their task. This obliges her to take care of everything. This makes her feel tired and oppressed. Giovanni, we learn, has never felt sufficiently valued by his parents, especially his father who imposed a tyrannical control over both his wife and children; he was always filled with anger and frustration, feelings which are still very active. He has a needy aspect, owing to lack of attention, which is expressed in 'sell, sell, sell', the insistence on obtruding his own products. Silvia too has experienced a lack of emotional recognition in her family environment, so as if to compensate for this she has built up a central role as director in which she makes herself indispensable, as if this were the only way to ensure her parents would notice her.

So what are the couple actually talking about? Integrating my own reflections with certain personal notes in each of theirs, we can understand the tensions in the relationship in terms of the psychic organisation of the couple, which has taken on a certain shape as a result of the bonding of their individual scenarios. We can perceive the crisscrossed circuit of projective identification in which each is engaged in living out a part of the other. For Giovanni, his wife seems to represent a primary object, organising him, putting him in the uncomfortable position of always having to ask for things. Silvia in a complementary way seems to accept this directorial role, moved by the fear that if she stopped she would be neglected and abandoned by her husband. For him, this confirms the idea of a constricting and suffocating figure who projects her own aggressiveness onto him.

This brief glimpse of a session illustrates what is an underlying theme in their roleplay. The couple's emotional bond is characterised by anxiety, by wanting recognition, and by impressionable and depressed aspects linked to the fear of not obtaining it. Later on during the therapy, our couple talk about how their quarrels take the form of provocations, threats, even physical violence, not unusually in front of the children. Giovanni recounts an episode in which he left a drawer open on purpose so his wife would hurt herself, which then actually happened. Another time Giovanni was told off by Silvia because the bread he was eating was placed too close to the edge of the table; he reacted by flinging the bread on the floor, treading on it and swearing with rage. Both episodes describe a reaction of uncontained violence. They seem to have no strategy of recovery; the arguments end up in the deepest reciprocal misunderstanding, with no subsequent moments of emotional recollection and digestion.

At one point in the session an opportunity emerged to make a comment about the shared dimension of the experiences being recounted. So I had the chance to make explicit how the moments of rage bring them in spite of themselves to crumble uncontrollably without finding anything to stop the avalanche, a condition which frightens them. I explained we need to appreciate and understand the feelings of rage and frustration but also make sure we limit their inappropriate and destructive expression.

Silvia and Giovanni have a hostile and violent relationship which they put me in a position of observing, indeed involving me more directly, by communicating their experiences of being threatened and their fear of their stress and suffering not being recognised. They make an impelling demand for answers, and ask in ways that seem to be defensive deformations of their original needs. The participatory role of the therapist thus comes under strain. My own transference experience is tense in character and I find myself needing to be very careful and cautious with my interventions. Sometimes there is even a collapse in my empathic abilities and I realise I am losing attention not only in relation to the argument but also in relation to the feelings of the couple. I wonder if this might be connected to aspects of my own family experience in which I frequently lived through situations of tension, conflict and direct aggression, against which I used to react by cutting off communication and blanking out the relationship as a method of defending myself. These defensive modes may have re-emerged in the intersubjective field of the couple therapy in the form of a partial or temporary disalignment, generating even more explosiveness in the partners, thereby perpetuating the absence of empathic response which is in fact the couple's primary anxiety.

Clinical work in this phase therefore lay in the regulation of explosive emotional tensions not only between them but between the three of us. In this situation of strong conflict, where signs of mentalisation were scarce, I felt it necessary in the first instance to establish emotional contact with the couple to understand the forces with which they were struggling, in order to begin to attempt to orchestrate the atmosphere in the field. Interpretation was from the beginning oriented towards their interactive dynamic as it presented itself during the session – to the reciprocity and quality of exchanges, including physical and nonverbal modes. Since within violent relationships the partners act out their own states of mind, and are also far from recognising them, it is necessary for the therapist to conduct his work with caution, identifying the appropriate level which the patients can access, whilst understanding the origin and significance of their actions. In this case I tried first to 'be with' the partners, engaging them in our shared task, and also to make sure they found a place as a couple in my own mind, seeing them as a joint entity who were in a continual state of fear of not being responded to in a punctual and appropriate manner.

The syntonic responsiveness of the therapist is different in the context of different treatments; it also varies within different sessions. The therapist, whose aim is to present the idea of a conjugal relationship, is engaged in managing his triangular situation, re-establishing contact or repairing ruptures between himself and the other, individually or together. He may welcome and legitimise the position of one partner, whilst limiting inappropriate expression, and always remaining in contact with the other. He translates the communication of the most vulnerable language of needs and desires, and he offers an empathic, calming containment of spontaneous expressions of emotion. He welcomes both differences and similarities between the partners, as capable of contributing usefully to the idea of the conjugal couple.

It becomes clearer to the couple that the object of their work is that of 'making an experience' of their own subjective reactions in conjunction with the therapist, who helps bring diverse interactive configurations into view. What happens in the session's *mise en scène* is a continuous roleplay (Sandler, 1976), through observation and experimentation, in which the therapist strategically offers his own reflective awareness to be explored in the service of a therapeutical process. To find oneself reflected in the mind of the therapist is an experience that for patients who have limited emotional repertoires (very frequent in the couples we meet these days) favours the development of integrational types of mental representation. Patients learn to experience themselves as subjects, whilst enhancing their self-reflective function as objects (Aron, 1996), thus integrating observational and experiential functions.

To take a final vignette from the work with Silvia and Giovanni: at the beginning of one of the later sessions, Giovanni starts by saying they arrived late because the wife hadn't turned up; he phoned but she didn't answer and this really irritated him. Silvia explains that because she didn't find her husband where they had agreed to meet, she became anxious and went away for a short time; she thought she had left her phone at home, but that if it came to the worst, they would just meet at the consulting room. She then added that looking in her pocket she realised she did have her phone in fact; in this way she was able to contact her husband to let him know the situation and thus calm him down.

This last scenario seems to delineate a transformational movement. The finding of an unexpected means of contact (the phone) seems to be mediated and promoted by the background of a therapeutical context, an environment where minds meet. This seems to refer back to the initial difficulty in making contact that was the background to the first session, and suggests the possibility of a more hopeful outcome.

Conclusions

The combined contribution of the English school of object relations and of American self-psychology has enabled the development of a psychoanalytic approach centred principally on the study of the processes that revolve around the partners not just between themselves but with their therapist, and which is defined as 'intersubjectivity'. Owing to continuing research into modes of affect regulation, the individuals have made available to them a spectrum of ways of engagement that can help them to give shape to the specific meanings of a relational situation. The intrapsychic phenomena are therefore inseparable from the process of relational influence and mutual regulation of affects. The affective strategies of each partner may have their genesis in the story of their own primal relations, but the mode in which the dyadic system unfolds and is restructured in the process of the circumstances of the relationship, is understandable only within their interaction at the present time. From a clinical point of the view the centre of gravity of observation has progressively shifted from individual psyches to what is happening between them in the intersubjective field, and this is determined also by the therapist, whose subjective response helps to construct an alternative system, orchestrating the meanings that arise during the session.

Different authors at different times have referred to the concept of 'interactive field' to highlight the usefulness of dynamic processes such as 'transactions', 'coupling', 'consonance', or 'reversible sequences and exchanges'. The concept of field is an attempt to overcome more static categories of objects and their representation, enriching the basic premises of the relational models and showing that they are still in process of construction within their diversified applications. Dynamic processes high-lighted by more heterogeneous therapeutic situations nonetheless converge with their originating models. In our experience the convergence of the two schools provides a methodology of great usefulness for the psychoanalytical treatment of couples, focusing as it does on the composition of the story during the sessions, by exploring the impact of emotional positions and narratives that are more adequate and functional than those currently employed by the couple. Then once the therapeutical space is internalised, they are able to offer each other psychological containment, relational intimacy and understanding.

Albasi C. (2007). *Attaccamenti Traumatici. I Modelli Operativi Interni Dissociati.* Novara: UTET.

Allen J. G., & Fonagy P. (2006). *Mentalization-based Treatment.* Chichester: Wiley & Sons.

Aron L. (1996). *A Meeting of Minds: Mutuality in Psychoanalysis,* Hilldale, N.J.: The Analytic Press.

Baranger M., & Baranger W. (1961–62). La situación analítica como campo dinámico (The analytic situation as a dynamic field), *Revista Uruguaya Psicoanálisis,* 4 (1): 3–54.

Beebe, B., & Lachman, F. (2002). *Infant research and adult treatment: Co-construing interactions.* Hillsdale, NJ: The Analytic Press.

Berman W. H., & Sperling, M. (1994). The structure and function of adult attachment. In: Berman W. H., & Sperling, M. (2004) *Attachment in Adults. Clinical and Developmental Perspectives.* New York: Guilford Press.

Bezoari, M., & Ferro A. (1991). Percorsi nel campo bi personale dell'analisi: dal gioco delle parti alle trasformazioni di coppia. *Rivista Italiana di Psicoanalisi,* 1: 5-47.

Bezoari M., & Ferro, A. (1994). Il posto del sogno all'interno di una teoria del campo analitico. *Rivista Italiana di Psicoanalisi,* 2: 251-72.

Bianchini B., & Dallanegra, L. (2010). Entre créativitè et violence: le contact des psychés dans la relation de couple; le divan familial. *Revue de Thérapie Familiale Psychanalytique*, 24: 97–107.

Bianchini, B., et al. (2009). Psicoterapia di coppia, psicoterapia di gruppo: una dialettica possibile? *Rivista Gruppi nella Clinica nelle Istituzioni, nella Società*, 1: 87–103. Milan: Franco Angeli.

Bianchini, B., & Dallanegra, L. (2011). Reflections on the container–contained model in couple psychoanalytic psychotherapy. *Couple and Family Psychoanalysis*, 1 (1): 69–80.

Bion, W. R. (1959). Attacks on linking. Reprinted in: *Second Thoughts*, pp. 93–109. London: Heinemann, 1967.

Bion, W. R. (1961). *Experiences in Groups*. London: Tavistock.

Bion, W. R. (1962). *Learning from Experience*. London: Heinemann.

Bion, W. R. (1963). *Elements of Psychoanalysis*. London: Heinemann.

Bion, W. R. (1965). *Transformations*. Heinemann,London.

Bion, W. R. (1970). *Attention and Interpretation*. London: Tavistock.

Bion, W. R. (1980). *Bion in New York and São Paulo*. Perthshire: Clunie Press.

Bion, W. R. (2005). *The Italian Seminars*. London: Karnac.

Bleger, J. (1967). *Simbiosis y ambigüedad, estudio psicoanalítico*, Editorial Paidós, Buenos Aires.

Bolognini, S. (2004). Intrapsychic–interpsychic. *International Journal of Psychoanalysis*, 85: 337-358.

Bolognini, S. (2008). *Passaggi Segreti. Teoria e Tecnica della Relazione Interpsichica*. Turin: Bollati Boringhieri.

Bordi, S. (1995). Lo stato attuale del concetto di neutralità analitica. *Rivista Italiana di Psicoanalisi*, 3: 373–390.

Bordi, S. (1996). *I Seminari milanesi di Sergio Bordi*. A cura del Direttivo del Centro Milanese di psicoanalisi, Milano.

Bowlby, J. (1979). Psychoanalysis as art and science. *International Review of Psychoanalysis*, 6: 3–14.

Bowlby, J. (1969–1982). *Attachment and Loss*. 3 vols. London: Hogarth Press.

Bowlby, J. (1988). *A Secure Base: Parent-Child Attachment and Healthy Human Development*. London: Routledge.

Britton, R. (1989). The missing link: parental sexuality in the Oedipus Complex. In: J. Steiner (Ed.), *The Oedipus Complex Today*, pp. 83–102. London: Karnac.

Britton, R. (2000). *Belief and Imagination*. London: Routledge.

Bromberg, P. M. (1993). Shadow and substance: a relational perspective on clinical process. *Psychoanalytic Psychology*, 10: 147–168.

Bromberg, P. M. (1998). *Standing in the Spaces: Essays on Clinical Process, Trauma, and Dissociation*. Hillsdale, N.J.: Analytic Press.

Caporali, P. (2010). Su alcune possibili estensioni del concetto di identificazione proiettiva. *Rivista Italiana di Psicoanalisi*, 4: 839–858.

Carli, R. (1993). *L'analisi della Domanda in Psicologia Clinica*. Milan: Giuffrè.

Carli L., Cavanna D., & Zavattini, G. C. (2009). *Psicologia delle Relazioni di Coppia*. Bologna: Il Mulino.

Castellano R., Velotti P., & Zavattini G. C. (2010). *Cosa ci fa Restare Insieme?*, Il Mulino, Bologna.

Civitarese, G. (2008). *L'Intima Stanza*. Rome: Borla.

Clulow, C. (2001). *Adult Attachment and Couple Psychotherapy*. London: Routledge.

Clulow, C. (2007). Can attachment theory help define what is mutative in couple psychoanalytic psychotherapy? In: Ludlam, M., & Nyberg, V., *Couple Attachment. Theoretical and Clinical Studies*, pp. 207–220. London: Karnac Books.

Clulow, C. (2009). (Ed.). *Sex, Attachment and Couple Psychotherapy: Psychoanalytic Perspectives*, Karnac Books, London.

Colman, W. (1993). Marriage as a Psychological Container. In: Ruszczynski, S., *Psychotherapy with Couples, Theory and Practice at the Tavistock Institute of Marital Studies*, pp. 70–98. London: Karnac.

Colman, W. (1995). Gesture and recognition: an alternative model to projective identification as a basis for couple relationships. In: Ruszczynski, S. (Ed.), *Intrusivenness and Intimacy in the Couple*, pp. 59-73. London: Karnac.

Corigliano, N. A. (Ed.) (1999). *Curare la Relazione: Saggi sulla Psicoanalisi e la Coppia*. Milan: Franco Angeli.

Dallanegra, L. (2007). La tutela del minore nel conflitto genitoriale della separazione: affido esclusivo, affido congiunto. Training course in Milan, 23 October.

Dazzi, N., & Zavattini G. C. (2011). Il paradigma dell'attaccamento e la pratica clinica. *Giornale Italiano di Psicologia*, 4: 729-756.

De Campora G., & Zavattini, G. C. (2011) Il bambino 'in relazione' con il mondo. In: Barbaglio, C. B., & Mondello, L. (Eds.),

Quaderni di Psicoterapia Infantile. Nuovi Assetti della Clinica Psicoanalitica in Età Evolutiva, 62: 35–65. Rome: Borla.

Dellarosa A., et al. (2008). (Eds.) *La Relazione e la Cura. Viaggio nel mondo della psicoterapia relazionale.* Milan: Franco Angeli.

Dicks, H.V. (1967). *Marital Tensions.* London: Routledge.

Eiguer A. (2008) *Jamais Moi sans Toi.* Paris: Dunod.

Emde, R. N. (1988). Development terminable and interminabile: innate and motivational factors from infancy. *International Journal of Psychoanalysis,* 69 (1): 23–42.

Emde, R. N. (1991). L'incrociarsi di tre strade: un cambiamento di punti di vista nella storia psicoanalitica di Edipo. In: Ammaniti, M., & Stern, D. (Eds.), *Rappresentazioni e Narrazioni,* pp. 98-112. Bari: Laterza.

Falone, D. (2004). La psicoanalisi nordamericana contemporanea. *Gli Argonauti,* 8: 7–20.

Ferro, A. (1992). *La Tecnica nella Psicoanalisi Infantile.* Milan: Cortina.

Ferro, A. (1993). Disegno, identificazione proiettiva e processi trasformativi, *Rivista Italiana di Psicoanalisi,* 4: 667–680.

Ferro, A. (2002a). *Seeds of Illness, Seeds of Recovery: The Genesis of Suffering and the Role of Psychoanalysis.* London: Routledge.

Ferro, A. (2002b). *In the Analyst's Consulting Roo m* [1996] trans. P. Slotkin. London: Routledge.

Ferro, A. (2005). Réflexions à propos de l'interprétation. *Bulletin de la Fédération Européenne de Psychanalyse,* 59: 44–46.

Ferro, A. (2006). Da una psicoanalisi dei contenuti e delle memorie a una psicoanalisi per gli apparati per sognare, sentire, pensare: transfert transfer trasferimenti. *Rivista di Psicoanalisi,* 2: 401–478.

Ferro, A. (2007). *Evitare le Emozioni, Vivere le Emozioni.* Milan: Cortina.

Ferro, A. (2008). Lavorare con le emozioni: che mestiere è? (Talk). Conference at Area G, Milan.

Ferro, A. (2009). Contenibilità ed incontenibilità delle emozioni. In: V. P. Pellicanò (Ed.), *Aggressività, Trasformazione e Contenimento.* Rome: Borla.

Ferro, A. (2010). Esplorazioni dell'inconscio: prospettive cliniche. (Talk). 15th Congress of the Italian Psychoanalytic Society (SPI). Taormina.

Ferro, A., & Vender, S. (2010) *La terra di nessuno fra psichiatria e psicoterapia.* Turin: Bollati Boringhieri.

Ferruta, A. (2011). Continuità e discontinuità tra narcisismo sano e patologico. Configurazioni oscillatorie. *Rivista Italiana di Psicoanalisi*, 1: 17–34.

Filippini, S., & Ponsi, M. (1993). Enactment. *Rivista Italiana di Psicoanalisi*, 3: 501–516.

Fisher, J. (1999). *The Uninvited Guest: Emerging from Narcisism towards Marriage*. London: Karnac.

Fisher, J., & Crandell, L. (2001). Patterns of relating in the couple. In: Clulow, C. (Ed.), *Adult Attachment and Couple Psychotherapy: The 'Secure Base' in Practice and Research*, pp. 15–27. London: Routledge.

Fonagy, P., & Target, M. (1997). Attachment and reflective function: their role in self-organization. *Development and Psychopathology*, 9: 679–700.

Fonagy P., et al. (2002). *Affect Regulation, Mentalization, and the Development of the Self*. New York: Other Press.

Freud, S. (1905). Three essays on the theory of sexuality. *Standard Edition 7*, pp. 135–245.

Freud, S. (1912). The dynamics of transference. *Standard Edition 12*, pp. 99–108

Freud, S. (1913). Totem and Taboo. *Standard Edition 13*, pp. vii–162.

Freud, S. (1915). Instincts and their vicissitudes. *Standard Edition 14*, pp. 111–140.

Freud, S. (1917). Metapsychology and other works. *Standard Edition 14*, pp. 237–258.

Freud, S. (1921). Group psychology and the analysis of the ego. *Standard Edition 18*, pp.69–143.

Gabbard, G. O., & Ogden, T. O. (2009). On becoming a psychoanalyst. *International Journal of Psychoanalysis*, 90: 311–327.

Gabbard G. O., & Westen, D. (2003). Rethinking therapeutic action. *International Journal of Psychoanalysis*, 84: 823–841.

Giannakoulas, A. (1992). La membrana diadica. *Interazioni Clinica e Ricerca Psicoanalitica su Individuo–Coppia–Famiglia*, I: 129–132. Milan: Franco Angeli.

Gigli, F., Velotti, P., Zavattini, G. C. (2012a). Working with couples between past and present: some clinical implications. *Couple and Family Psychoanalysis*, 2: 65–79.

Gigli, F., Velotti, P., & Zavattini, G. C. (2012b). Concreción y mentalización: articulaciones de un camino psicoanalítico. *Psicoanalisis & Intersubjetividad*. www.intersubjetividad.com.ar.

Gosling, R. (1968). What is Transference. In: J. Sutherland, *The Psychoanalytic Approach*, pp. 1–10. London: Baillere, Tindall & Cassell.

Grier, F. (2001). (Ed.). *Brief Encounters with Couples: Some Analytical Perspectives*. Karnac Books, London.

Grier, F. (2005). (Ed.). *Oedipus and the Couple*. London: Karnac.

Grinberg, L. (1981). *Psicoanalisis: Aspectos Teoricos y Clinicos*. Barcelona: Paidos.

Grotstein, J. S. (1981). *Splitting and Projective Identification*. New York: Aronson.

Grotstein, J. S. (2007). *A Beam of Intense Darkness*. London: Karnac.

Hartmann, H. (1950). Comments on the psychoanalytic theory of the ego. *Psychoanalytic Study of the Child*, 5: 74–95.

Hughes, A. D. (2007). *Attachment-Focused Family Therapy*. New York: Norton.

Jacobson, E. (1954). The self and the object world: vicissitudes of their infantile cathexes and their influence on ideational and affective development. *Psychoanalytic Study of the Child*, 9: 75–127.

Jiménez, J.P. (2006). After pluralism: towards a new, integrated psychoanalytic paradigm. *International Journal of Psychoanalysis*, 87: 1487-1507.

Kaës, R. (2001). Il concetto di legame. *Ricerca Psicoanalitica*, 12 (2): 161–184.

Kaës, R. (2002). *La Polyphonie du Rêve: L'Espace Onirique Commun et Partagé*. Paris, Dunod.

Kernberg, O. F. (1995). *Love Relations*. New Yaven: Yale University Press.

Kernberg, O. F. (2011). Divergent contemporary trends in psychoanalytic theory. *The Psychoanalytic Review*, 98 (5): 633–664.

Klein, G. S. (1976). *Psychoanalytic Theory: An Exploration of Essentials*. New York: Basic Books.

Klein, M. (1928). Early stages of the Oedipus conflict. *International Journal of Psychoanalysis*, 9: 167–180.

Klein, M. (1946). Notes on some schizoid mechanisms. *International Journal of Psychoanalysis*, 27(3): 99–110.

Klein, M. (1948). *Contributions to Psychoanalysis 1921–1945*. London: Hogarth Press.

Klein, M. (1955). On identification. In: *Envy and Gratitude and Other Works*, pp. 141–171. London: Hogarth Press, 1979.

Klein, M. (1963) On the sense of loneliness. In: *Our Adult World and Other Essays*. London: Heinemann.

Klein, M., et al. (1952). *Developments in Psychoanalysis*. London: Hogarth Press.

Laing, R. D. (1961) *Self and Others*. London: Tavistock.

Laplanche, J., & Pontalis, G. B. (1968). *Vocabulaire de la Psychoanalyse*. Puf, Paris.

Lemaire, J. G. (1979). Le Couple, sa Vie sa Mort. Paris: Payot.

Lingiardi, V., et al. (2011). *La Svolta Relazionale*. Milan: Cortina.

Loewald, H. (1979). The waning of the Oedipus complex. In: *Papers on Psychoanalysis*, pp. 384–404. New Haven: Yale University Press, 1980.

Losso, R., & Packciarz Losso, A. (2000). La psicoanalisi e la coppia. In Losso, R., *Psicoanalisi della Famiglia*. Milan: Franco Angeli.

Lupinacci, M. A. (1994). Riflettendo sull'Edipo precoce: la coppia genitoriale nel lavoro dell'analista. *Rivista Italiana di Psicoanalisi*, 1: 5–23.

Lupinacci, M. A., & Zavattini, G. C. (2002). One dream for two people: dreaming in the psychoanalytic couple psychotherapy. *Funzione Gamma*. www.funzionegamma.edu.

Lupinacci, M. A, & Zavattini, G. C. (2004). La coppia come paziente. (Talk). Centro Psicoanalitico di Firenze, 12 March.

Lupinacci, M. A. (2012). Female elements and functions in creativity. (Talk). COWAP conference on *Women and Creativity*. 28–29 September, Genoa.

Mangini, E. (2003). (Ed.). *Lezioni sul Pensiero Post-Freudiano*. Milan: Edizioni Universitarie di Lettere Economia Diritto.

Meltzer, D. (1967). *The Psychoanalytic Process*. London: Heinemann.

Meltzer, D. (1992). *The Claustrum. An Investigation of Claustrophobic Phenomena*. Perthshire: Clunie Press.

Meltzer, D. & Williams, M. H. (1988). *The Apprehension of Beauty*. Perthshire: Clunie Press.

Merleau-Ponty, M. (1951). Les relations avec autrui chez l'enfant. In: *The Phenomenology of Perception*, ed. J. Edie, pp. 96–155. Evanston: Northwestern University Press, 1964.

Messina S., & Zavattini, G. C. (2008). Il senso della relazione: note sull'interpretazione. In: Nicolini, E. (Ed.), *Quaderni di Psicoterapia Psicoanalitica. Coppia e Famiglia in Psicoanalisi*, pp. 93–103. Rome: Borla.

Mitchell, S. (1988). *Relational Concepts in Psychoanalysis*. Cambridge, M.A.: Harvard University Press.

Mitchell, S., & Aron, L. (1999). *Relational Psychoanalisis – The emergence of a tradition*. Hillsdale, N.J.: Analytic Press.

Mitchell, S. (2000) *Relationality: From Attachment to Intersubjectivity.* Hillsdale, N.J.: Analytic Press.

Money-Kyrle, R. (1961). *Man's Picture of his World.* London: Duckworth. New edition: Harris Meltzer Trust, 2015.

Monguzzi F. (2010). *Curare la Coppia. Processi Terapeutici e Fattori Mutativi.* Milan: Franco Angeli.

Morgan, M., & Ruszczynski, S. (1998). The creative couple. (Talk). Tavistock Marital Studies Institute 50th Anniversary Conference.

Morgan, M. (2001). First contacts: the therapist's 'couple state of mind' as a factor in the containment of couples seen for consultations. In: Grier, F. (Ed.), *Brief Encounters with Couples: Some Analytical Perspectives*, pp. 7–32.

Morgan, M. (2005). On being able to be a couple: the importance of a 'creative couple' in psychic life, In: Grier F. (Ed.), *Oedipus and the Couple*, pp. 9–30. London: Karnac.

Nebbiosi, G. (2008). Psicoanalisi e istituti psicoanalitici indipendenti. *Interazioni*, 2 (30): 11–29.

Neri, C. (2007). La nozione allargata di campo in psicoanalisi. In: Ferro, A., & Basile, R. (Eds.), *Il Campo Analitico*. Rome: Borla, 2011.

Norsa, D. (2007). Intimacy, collusion and complicity in psychotherapy with couples. *Revue Internationale de Psychanalyse du Couple et de la Famille*, 2007 (2): 152–163.

Norsa, D., & Zavattini, G. C. (1997). *Intimità e Collusione. Teoria Tecnica della Psicoterapia Psicoanalitica di Coppia.* Milan: Cortina.

Ogden, T. H. (1979). On projective identification, *International Journal of Psychoanalysis*, 60: 357–72.

Ogden, T. H. (1992). The dialectically decentred subject of psychoanalysis: the contribution of Klein and Winnicott. *International Journal of Psychoanalysis*, 73: 613–626.

Ogden, T. H. (1994). The analytic third: working with intersubjective clinical facts. In: *Subjects of Analysis*, pp. 61–96. London: Karnac.

Ogden, T. H. (1997). Reverie and interpretation. *The Psychoanalytic Quarterly*, 66: 567–597.

Ogden, T. H. (2004). On holding and containing, being and dreaming,

International Journal of Psychoanalysis, 85: 1349–1364.

Ogden, T. H. (2005). *This Art of Psychoanalysis: Dreaming Undreamt Dreams and Interrupted Cries*. London: Routledge.

Ogden, T. H. (2009). *Rediscovering Psychoanalysis: Thinking and Dreaming, Learning and Forgetting*. Hove: Routledge.

Pellicanò, V. P. (2009). (Ed.). *Aggressività, Trasformazione e Contenimento*. Rome: Borla.

Pickering, J. (2011). Bion and the Couple. *Couple and Family Psychoanalysis*, 1(1): 49–68.

Pincus, L. (1960). (Ed.). *Marriage: Studies in Emotional Conflict and Growth*. London: Tavistock.

Puget, J. (2010). The subjectivity of certainty and the subjectivity of uncertainty. *Psychoanalytic Dialogues*, 20: 4–20.

Putnam, F. (1992). Discussion: are alter personalities fragments or figments? In: Bromberg, P. M. (Ed.), *Clinica del Trauma e della Dissociazione*. Italian transl. Milan: Cortina.

Riviere, Joan (1952). The inner world as seen in literature. In: A. Hughes (Ed.), *The Inner World and Joan Riviere: Collected Papers 1929-1958*, pp. 310 –148. London: Karnac, 1991.

Rouchy, J. C. (1998). *Le Group, Espace Analytique Clinique et Théorie*. Paris: Edition Erès.

Ruszczynski, S. (1992). Some notes towards a psychoanalytic understanding of couple relationships. *Psychoanalytic Psychotherapy*, 6: 33–44.

Ruszczynski, S. (1993). (Ed.), *Psychotherapy with Couples: Theory and Practice at the Tavistock Institute of Marital Studies*. London: Karnac.

Ruszczynski, S. (1996). L'Edipo rivisitato: le induzioni transferali nella psicoterapia psicoanalitica della coppia. *Interazioni, 2* (8):11–26.

Ruszczynski, S. (2005). Reflective space in the intimate couple relationship : the 'marital triangle'. In: F. Grier (Ed.), *Oedipus and the Couple*, pp. 31–48. London: Karnac.

Ruszczynski, S., & Fisher, J. (1995). *Intrusivenness and Intimacy in the Couple*. London: Karnac.

Sameroff, A. J., & Emde, R. N. (1989))(Eds.), *Relationship Disturbances in Early Childhood: A developmental Approach*. New York: Basic Books.

Sandler, J. (1976). Countertransference and role-responsiveness.

*International Review of Psychoanaly*sis, 3: 43–47.

Santona, A., & Zavattini, G. C. (2005). Ni avec toi, ni sans toi: collusion et accordage affective dans le couple. *Le divan familial*, 14: 39–47.

Santona, A., & Zavattini, G. C. (2007). *La Relazione di Coppia*, Borla, Roma, 2007.

Santona, A., & Zavattini, G. C. (2008). Intersoggettività e reciprocità nella psicoterapia di coppia. In: Chianura P., et al. (Eds.), *Le Relazioni e la Cura: Viaggio nel Mondo della Psicoterapia Relazionale*. Milan: Franco Angeli.

Scharff, D. E., & Scharff, J. S. (1991). *Object Couple Therapy*. Northvale, N. J.: Aronson.

Scharff, D. E. (2011) The concept of the link in psychoanalytic therapy. *Couple and Family Psychoanalysis*, 1, 34-48.

Segal, H. (1964) *Introduction to the Work of Melanie Klein*. London: Maresfield.

Selvini Palazzoli, M., et al. (1975). *Paradosso e Contro Paradosso*. Milan: Feltrinelli.

Shaddock, D. (2000). *Contexts and Connections: An Intersubjective Systems Approach to Couples Therapy*. New York: Basic Books.

Steiner, J. (1993). *Psychic Retreats*. London Routledge.

Stern, D. N. (1985). *The Interpersonal World of the Infant*. London: Karnac.

Stern, D. N. (1989). The representation of relational patterns: developmental considerations. In: Sameroff, A. J., & Emde, R.N. (Eds.), *I Disturbi della Relazione nella Prima Infanzia*. Italian trans. Turin: Bollati Boringhieri, 1991.

Stern D. N. (1995). *The Motherhood Constellation: A Unified View of Parent–Infant Psychotherapy*. New York: Basic Books.

Stern D.N. (2004). *The Present Moment in Psychotherapy and Everyday Life*. New York: Norton.

Stern, D. (2005). Intersubjectivity. In: Person, E. S., et al. (Eds.), *Textbook of Psychoanalysis*, pp. 79–92. Washington, D.C.: American Psychiatric Publishing.

Stolorow, R., & Atwood, G. E. (1992). *Contexts of Being: The Intersubjective Foundations of Psychological Life*. Hillsdale, N.J.: The Analytic Press.

Stolorow, R., et al. (1994) (Eds.) *The Intersubjective Perspective*. Northvale, N.J.: Aronson.

Sullivan, H. S. (1940). Conceptions of modern psychiatry: the first William Alanson White Memorial Lectures. *Psychiatry,* 3: 1–17.

Sullivan, H.S . (1953). *The Interpersonal Theory of Psychiatry.* New York: Norton.

Tabbia, C. (2008). El concepto de intimidad en el pensamento de Meltzer. (Talk). Conference on *O Pensamento Vivo de Donald Meltzer.* Sao Paulo, Brazil.

Tabbia, C. (2010). Appunti psicoanalitici sull'invidia. (Talk). Centro Choros, Savona, May.

Teruel, G. (1966). Considerations for a diagnosis in marital psychotherapy, *British Journal of Medical Psychology,* 39 (3): 231–236.

Velotti, P., & Zavattini, G. C. (2008). The encounter with the other in the couple relationship: the area of mutuality. *Funzione Gamma,* 21 (March). www.funzionegamma.edu.

Velotti, P., Castellano R., & Zavattini G. C. (2011). Adjustment of couples following childbirth. *European Psychologist,* 16 (1): 1–11.

Winnicott, D. W. (1957). On the capacity to be alone. *International Journal of Psychoanalysis,* 39: 416–420.

Winnicott, D.W. (1958) *Through Paediatrics to Psychoanalysis.* New York: Basic Books.

Winnicott, D. W. (1961). The theory of the parent-infant relationship. *International Journal of Psychoanalysis,* 41: 585–595.

Winnicott D. W. (1965). *The Maturational Processes and the Facilitating Environment.* London: Hogarth Press.

Wolff, P. H. (1987). *The Development of Behavioral States and the Expression of Emotion in Early Infancy.* Chicago: University of Chicago Press.

Zaccagnini, C., et al. (2008). Relazione di coppia e funzione riflessiva. In: Santona, A., & Zavattini, G. C., *La Relazine di Coppia.* Rome: Borla.

Zavattini G. C. (1988). Dall'analista specchio al campo bipersonale: il setting come contenitore della relazione terapeutica. In: Colamonico, P., & Lombardo, G. P. (Eds.), *Malattia e Psicoterapia: Identità, Specificità e Responsabilità nell'Intervento dello Psicologo Clinico*, pp. 267–281. Roma: Bulzoni.

Zavattini, G. C. (1988). L'altro di me, ovvero la mia metà: considerazioni sull'identificazione proiettiva. *Rivista Italiana di Psicoanalisi,* 2: 349–375.

Zavattini G. C., (1998). Il setting nella terapia psicoanalitica di coppia. *Rivista di Psicoterapia Relazionale*, 7: 23–40.

Zavattini, G. C. (2001a). Shared internal worlds: collusion and affect attunement in the couple. *Bullettin of the Society of Psychoanalytical Marital Psychotherapists*, 8: 29–36.

Zavattini, G. C. (2001 b). Collusione e riparazione nelle relazioni di coppia. *Psicoterapia Psicoanalitica*, 2: 62–73.

Zavattini, G. C. (2004). Interpretazione, transfert e controtransfert nel lavoro psicoanalitico con le coppie. (Talk). Centro Psicoanalitico di Bologna, 4 November.

Zavattini, G. C. (2005). Teoria e clinica nella terapia psicoanalitica di coppia. (Talk). Centro Arcipelago, Milano.

Zavattini, G. C. (2006). El 'espacio triangular' y el setting en la psicoterapia psicoanalitica de pareja. [2004]. *Psicoanalisis & Intersubjetividad*. www.intersubjetividad.com.ar.

Zavattini, G. C. (2008). The place of the unconscious is not only the individual mind: a comparison of models, *Funzione Gamma* 21: 1–5. www.funzionegamma.edu.

Zavattini, G. C., & Gigli, F. (2010). The couple link between tradition and modernity. (Talk). IACFP congress on *Couple and Family Psychoanalysis*, Buenos Aires, July 28–30.

Zavattini, G. C., et al. (2010). Attaccamento adulto e 'matching' di coppia. *Infanzia e Adolescenza*, 1: 39–52.

Zucconi, S. (2004). L'interazione transfert–controtransfert rivisitata. *Quaderni degli Argonauti*, 8: 93–112.